Property of Sr. B. Michael N.D.

D1483715

America's Vietnam Policy

THE STRATEGY OF DECEPTION

"Every violation of truth is not only a sort of suicide in the liar, but is a stab at the health of human society."—Ralph Waldo Emerson.

* * * *

"The very foundation of the democratic system is built on honesty and the belief in the honesty of our fellow men . . . Yet the political lie has become a way of bureaucratic life. It has been called by the more genteel name of 'news management.' I say here now, let's call it what it is—lying.

"I would like to suggest that one of the reasons for the great confusion which wracks this nation today over the Vietnam War is the fact that we were committed without a proper airing of the facts—all the facts. This Administration and preceding ones did not level with the American people on the nature or scope of the commitment which, I submit, they themselves must have known was one of the ultimates of our policy."—Walter Cronkite, CBS News, in speech before Inland Press Association, Feb. 23, 1966.

* * * *

"Today it seems to me, as it has for many months, that the pressure of events is remorselessly leading toward a major war, while efforts to reverse that trend are lagging disastrously behind. In my view the tragic error is being repeated of relying on force and military means in a deceptive pursuit of peace."—U.N. Secretary General U Thant, Sept. 1, 1966.

America's Vietnam Policy

THE STRATEGY OF DECEPTION

By Edward S. Herman
and Richard B. Du Boff

Public Affairs Press, Washington, D. C.

PREFACE

The American people have not been told the truth about our current Vietnam involvement. That more than anything else is the reason why there is mounting confusion and uneasiness among all segments of our population. The inconsistencies between Washington's actions and professed aims, and between its appeals to loyalty and trust and its heavy reliance on deception, have contributed to widespread feelings of frustration, bewilderment, and anger. Official pronouncements and subsequent disclosures of fact have conflicted so often that, as James Reston has observed, a major casualty of the war may well be "confidence in the good judgment and good faith of the United States government."

To help keep the opposition to this "unwanted war" within manageable bounds, government officials have applied an impressive array of public relations techniques to all aspects of the war. At the same time they have enforced a system of news controls that, in the words of Wes Gallagher, general manager of Associated Press, "exceed anything done during the darkest days of World War II." The citizen's right to accurate information has been treated with open disdain. Carl Rowan, while head of the U.S. Information Agency, went so far as to proclaim "the public's right *not* to know." His lead has been followed by officials throughout the government. One of them, Assistant Secretary of Defense for Public Affairs Arthur Sylvester, told a group of American reporters in Saigon in July 1965 that their proper role was to serve as "handmaidens" of the government. The chief public information officer of the Pentagon then went on to say: "Look, if you think any American official is going to tell the truth, then you're stupid. Did you hear that?—stupid."

In view of these developments, there is a pressing need for a systematic analysis that attempts to reconcile the words and deeds of our Vietnam policy makers. The present volume represents an effort to fill this gap. It draws together a considerable body of information on the positions taken and the actions car-

5

ried out by the United States (and its antagonists), and seeks to identify the real obstacles to peace in Vietnam.

While particular attention is paid to Washington's stance toward negotiations since escalation of the war to North Vietnam early in 1965, such related matters as the aims of the administration, its strategy of escalation, and the earlier history of U.S. diplomacy in Vietnam are also examined.

The four appendices that follow the main text carry our analysis further, by allowing us to consider several specific questions raised by American policies. The first three review the principal claims of President Johnson, Secretary of State Rusk, and other high officials with respect to our goals in Vietnam: that we are fighting to safeguard international law for the world community and self-determination for the Vietnamese people; that we desire to protect the independence of South Vietnam; and that we are resisting aggression by North Vietnam. The fourth appendix is an appraisal of the potential results of U.S. military actions under the unique circumstances of a savagely contested guerrilla war.

Except for some discussion in Chapters II and III and Appendices 2 and 3, we make no attempt to deal with the fundamental issue of "why we got involved" in Vietnam in the first place. That vital question goes to the roots of U.S. foreign policy since World War II and, in turn, to all the political and economic forces that shape it.

We wish to acknowledge the helpful criticism and suggestions we received from friends and colleagues in the course of preparing this book. We owe thanks also to the Pennsylvania Universities Council on Problems of War and Peace. The Council sponsored the mimeographed version of the first draft of our manuscript, completed in January 1966.

Unless otherwise indicated, we have added the emphases (italics) in quotations used in this work.

E.S.H. AND R.B.D.

Philadelphia, Pa.

CONTENTS

I

Introduction 9

II

The Official Aims of the United States 15

III

The Logic of Escalation 31

IV

The Diplomacy of a "Win Policy" (1) 35

V

The Diplomacy of a "Win Policy" (2) 56

VI

Summary and Conclusions 76

APPENDIX 1

The Failure to Hold Elections in 1956 82

APPENDIX 2

Independence 89

APPENDIX 3

Aggression By Whom? 96

APPENDIX 4

Genocide in Vietnam? 114

planned extermination of an entire people or country

ABOUT THE AUTHORS

Edward S. Herman received a Ph.D. in economics from
the University of California. He has held teaching and
research positions at a number of colleges and universities, including the University of California, Pennsylvania
State, and, since 1958, the University of Pennsylvania,
where he is Associate Professor of Finance.

A long-time student of public policy issues, he has
written articles on international relations and economic
trends and has held a Ford Faculty Research Fellowship.

Richard B. Du Boff received his B.A. from Dartmouth
College and his Ph.D. from the University of Pennsyl-
vania. At the present time he is Assistant Professor of
Economics at Bryn Mawr College.

He is a member of the Inter-University Committee for
Debate on Foreign Policy and has contributed articles on
international affairs to both domestic and foreign jour-
nals. His areas of specialization are economic history
and contemporary economic systems. He has held fel-
lowships from both the National Science Foundation
and Resources for the Future, Inc.

I

INTRODUCTION

The Johnson administration has encountered a "credibility gap" in many areas of its Vietnam policy. But nowhere has this problem been more severe than in Washington's claims of a deep interest in a negotiated settlement of the war in Vietnam. Here credibility has been impaired by the fact that at first the administration did not even pretend that it sought negotiations before escalating the war to North Vietnam in February 1965. It was not until March and April of that year that President Johnson expressed any interest at all in a negotiated settlement.

Furthermore, with the Sevareid-Stevenson revelations and other disclosures late in 1965, the American public finally learned that our government had refused outright to *discuss*, let alone negotiate, a settlement with Hanoi or the National Liberation Front (NLF) prior to the February 1965 escalation.[1] The State Department then acknowledged that in September 1964, and again after the November elections, Secretary-General U Thant's overtures to the United States to participate in a conference, to which Hanoi had agreed to come, were rejected in favor of a policy of unilateral force. Thus President Johnson's statement of July 28, 1965, that "We are ready now, *as we have always been,* to move from the battlefield to the conference table," was admitted to have been far less than the truth.

Yet despite this record of duplicity and misrepresentation, many people have been persuaded that the President's Johns Hopkins University speech of April 7, 1965 inaugurated a "new era" in which the administration, now sincerely interested in a

---

[1] When U Thant told a press conference on Feb. 24, 1965 that "I am sure that the great American people, if only they knew the true facts and the background to the developments in South Vietnam, will agree with me that further bloodshed is unnecessary," there is little doubt that he was referring to the Johnson administration's unwillingness to negotiate—and to its suppression of that fact.

negotiated settlement, was frustrated at every turn by an intransigent and uncooperative Hanoi. James Reston referred to the pre-April 7 period as the time "when President Johnson was stubbornly refusing to define his war aims in Vietnam, and rejecting all thought of a negotiated settlement . . ."; this he contrasted with the new era (April 7 and after) in which "The problem of peace lies now not in Washington but in Hanoi . . ."[2] Thus it was concluded, with official encouragement, that protests against the Johnson policies are not merely pointless, but may have the boomerang effect of deceiving Hanoi into underestimating Washington's resolve.

One of the many remarkable features of this new era view is the generally uncritical acceptance of words that are unsupported by corresponding actions. If we attempt to infer the purposes of the Johnson administration from its *deeds* (which we have always self-righteously demanded of the Communists, to demonstrate *their* sincerity), then the steady escalation of the war suggests the pursuit of a settlement imposed by force—that is, what the Goldwaterites have termed a "win policy." This conclusion is supported as well by the continued refusal of the United States, which initially chose "quantum" escalation rather than discussions, to take any meaningful steps toward a negotiated settlement.[3]

Furthermore, if we may judge the intentions of the Johnson administration from the *consequences* of escalation, then one of those intentions seems to have been to drive North Vietnam away from the conference table; for in all probability the bombings have had the effect of reducing Hanoi's willingness to negotiate. Such an effect must have been one of the purposes or acceptable costs of the bombings. (The alternative is that the administration made another catastrophic error in judgment.) If we can assume that the enemy response has been correctly understood by the U. S. government, this suggests the further possibility that our "peace moves" were extended only

---

[2] *New York Times*, Oct. 18, 1965.

[3] We show later that neither the five day lull in the bombing of North Vietnam in May 1965 nor the "peace offensive" of December 1965-January 1966 can be regarded as serious attempts to bring about negotiations.

because conditions had already been created that helped make
them unacceptable. This view is not a novel one in the nation's
capital. Robert Roth, Washington bureau chief of the *Philadelphia Bulletin,* reported on September 26, 1965 that "There are
some here—and they are not 'outsiders'—who maintain that
the Johnson administration . . . never wanted or intended to
negotiate and that *conferences were asked for because it was
reasonably certain that the Communists . . . would not agree
to them.*"

Since the actions of the United States in Vietnam have
been almost uniformly to expand the scope of the war, and
since its fuzzy and contradictory peace moves have been made
only after the feasibility of negotiations had been sharply reduced
by administration actions, it is surprising that so little attention
has been paid to the hypothesis that *Washington's peaceable
words have been solely for public relations effect.*[4] Put in another
way, it is possible that Hanoi *has* "got the message," and that
it is the American people who have been taken in by the deceptive cooing of an eagle fighting to win. If this hypothesis is
correct, then it is not the protesters against our Vietnam policy,
but its supporters who have been contributing to a prolonga-
tion and expansion of the war. They have been helping to
perpetrate a fraud which has enabled the Johnson administra-

---

[4] The importance of distinguishing between the words and deeds
of the Johnson administration is equally apparent in analyzing its
Dominican intervention. In his article on "The Dominican Crisis,"
Theodore Draper points out that "In order to follow the official
U.S. reaction to the April 24 revolt, it is necessary to move on two
levels: what U.S. officials *said,* and what U.S. officials privately *did*
. . . The difference between what President Johnson *said* about the
'popular democratic revolution that was committed to democracy
and social justice' and what was *done* about it has become almost
incredibly grotesque." (*Commentary,* Dec. 1965.)

[5] It is often urged against the Vietnam war protesters that President Johnson's policy is somehow a sanctified product of the "democratic consensus." Apart from the other objections to this argument, it neglects the fact that Johnson campaigned as the "peace"
candidate in 1964 against the allegedly irresponsible Barry Goldwater. Charles Roberts asserts in his book *LBJ's Inner Circle*
(New York, 1965, pp. 20-22) that Johnson had already planned to
escalate the war to North Vietnam by October 1964—at the very

tion to gull the American public into accepting Barry Goldwater's policy.[5]

We show in detail in this book that neither the Johns Hopkins speech of April 7, 1965, nor any subsequent administration peace move up to the present time, was *intended* to bring about a negotiated settlement in Vietnam. On the contrary, these efforts seem to have been directed exclusively to influencing domestic and foreign opinion.[6] In every aspect of their formulation and execution they show a *purposeful impracticality* as devices for bringing about a peaceful settlement of the war. On the other hand, they have been well designed for keeping the doves in a state of confused disarray; they have functioned as a safety valve to reduce pressures which otherwise might have compelled Washington to make the concessions to political reality necessary for a negotiated settlement.

A mass of new evidence made available in the 1966 hearings of the Senate Foreign Relations Committee and in official responses to Senator Robert Kennedy's proposal of February 2, 1966,[7] fully confirms our theses regarding the objectives of the Johnson administration and the public relations function of its peace moves. It has become quite clear that the administration never contemplated any compromises with the NLF or North Vietnam, and that at no time has it been interested in negotiations in

---

moment he was denouncing the "trigger happy" Goldwater and telling the American people that if elected he (Johnson) would "not go North and not go South" in Vietnam, and that he "knew of no plans that had been made" to extend the war to North Vietnam. Furthermore, the *New York Times* stated editorially (May 20, 1966) that the decision to bomb North Vietnam may even have been made earlier: "In the summer of 1964 Premier Khanh [of South Vietnam] was promised a bombing offensive against the North, presumably on presidential authority, to extract pledges from Saigon of governmental stability and efficacity."

This means that, aside from the manipulative aspects of the present "consensus" (discussed elsewhere in this book), Johnson's election victory rested upon a deception of the American public and thus on an abuse of the democratic process.

[6] Joseph Alsop apparently also holds this view. He has written: "The truth is that the President made his original offer of 'unconditional' negotiations, and has since repeated that offer for the main purpose of disarming the domestic and foreign critics of his Viet-

any meaningful sense of the term; for all practical purposes it has merely used that word to describe a conference that would "ratify the end of the Communist threat to South Vietnam . . ."[8] As Senator Fulbright has put it, "Our objective seems to be the surrender of North Vietnam, and that means we will do anything necessary for victory rather than compromise."[9] More recently, Walter Lippmann concluded in regard to the Johnson policy:

"From the President's press conference [June 18, 1966] . . . it is now clear that he still hopes for a solution in Vietnam by military victory. He has not quite said what General Ky said over the weekend—that the Vietcong would be defeated in a year.

"But he did say that he expects to defeat the fighting forces of the enemy and compel him to negotiate a peace *on our terms.*

"For the time being, until the test of battle has been gone through, he will make none of the concessions which are the essential ingredients of a negotiated peace."[10]

Although all of this has become more evident in recent months, one may be certain that as the disaster in Vietnam is enlarged,

nam policy." ("The Negotiations Nonsense," *New York Herald Tribune*, Nov. 19, 1965.)

Writing for the *Wall Street Journal* just after conferring with administration officials in late 1965, William Beecher stated: "The negotiation chant served administration designs quite well. It helped quiet criticism, both domestic and foreign, about our 'militaristic' policy in Vietnam. And, at a time when we were launching a mammoth buildup of combat forces, constant talk of negotiations also served to allay the fears of Hanoi, Peking, and Moscow about an ultimate U.S. invasion of the North and a forced reunification of the two Vietnams. For such benefits as these, some lip service to negotiation ought to continue." (Oct. 14, 1965.)

[7] A proposal to negotiate directly with the NLF and admit it to a coalition Saigon government before elections take place.

[8] Max Frankel, "New Light on U.S. Policy," *New York Times*, Feb. 18, 1966.

[9] *New York Times*, March 4, 1966.

[10] "President Puts Chips on Military Victory," *Philadelphia Inquirer*, June 21, 1966 (emphasis in original).

the administration will justify its actions, as it has in the past, by resorting to the argument that "we were simply unable to persuade the enemy to 'negotiate'." We therefore feel it necessary to spell out in detail the misleading character of this argument (and others related to it).

The meaning of the "peace" moves of the Johnson administration may be understood from an analysis of: (1) the stated and implied purposes of the United States in Vietnam, and the conditions necessary for their fulfillment; (2) the logic of the policy of escalation; (3) the background of American diplomacy in Vietnam, the timing and character of the principal administration peace moves, and the handling of enemy responses to these efforts. We turn to a consideration of these issues.

THE OFFICIAL AIMS OF THE U. S.

Ever since the fall of 1954 when the United States replaced a defeated France as the Western "presence" in Indochina, its primary aim there has been to maintain what President Johnson and his predecessors have referred to as the "independence of South Vietnam." Unfortunately for the legality and morality of the American position in Vietnam, the Geneva Accords of July 1954, which formally ended the eight-year French-Vietminh war, *did not partition Vietnam into two separate and independent nations.*

The Geneva Agreements state clearly that the 17th parallel (now the *de facto* boundary between North and South Vietnam) was a "provisional military demarcation line" that "should not in any way be interpreted as constituting a political or territorial boundary" (Articles 1 and 8; Article 6 of the Final Declaration). The 17th parallel temporarily divided Vietnam into two "regrouping zones," the unification of which was to take place by "free general elections" scheduled for July 1956. Therefore, the persistent American claims to be defending an independent nation, to be safeguarding its autonomy, fly in the face of every explicit provision of the Geneva Accords.[1] In addition,

---

[1] It is worth noting that in the *entire* 47 articles and Final Declaration of the Geneva Accords there is no mention whatsoever of the two "independent" nations, North and South Vietnam. The political theme of the Accords is *unification* of the country.

A particularly lucid illustration of the many official misrepresentations of the content of the Geneva Accords is the following statement by Secretary Rusk: "The other side was fully committed—fully committed—in the original Geneva settlement of 1954 to the arrangements *which provided for South Vietnam as an independent entity* . . ." (*New York Times*, Dec. 9, 1963). This misrepresentation was repeated by President Johnson in his statement before the American Bar Association on Aug. 12, 1964, that the Geneva Agreements "guaranteed the independence of South Vietnam."

15

Geneva

they contradict the 1954 pledge that "In the case of nations now divided against their will, we shall continue to seek to achieve unity through free elections supervised by the United Nations to insure that they are conducted fairly."[2]

It is important to recognize that in reference to South Vietnam, "independent" is employed by spokesmen for the United States in an Orwellian sense, synonymous with "non-Communist and attached to our side." According to this usage, General Ky, President Ngo Dinh Diem, and Bao Dai are (or were) "independent," whatever their degree of subservience to the United States or France; on the other hand, the NLF and Ho Chi Minh can never be "independent," whatever their degree of national autonomy or popular support.[3] Free elections and self-determination in Vietnam have always seemed incompatible with this conception of "independence," and the United States has always been unenthusiastic about their application in that country. President Eisenhower, although acknowledging that in 1954 he

---

Mr. Rusk contradicted himself on this point in 1966, simultaneously adding another distortion to conform to the current U.S. position. During the Senate Foreign Relations Committee hearings in February 1966, he stated that the Geneva Accords "did not establish [Vietnam] as two separate nations, but it did provide some procedures by which this could occur *if that is what the people wanted.*" The italicized language is the new distortion: Article Seven of the Final Declaration at Geneva calls for unifying elections without any qualifications such as Rusk now attached. For a discussion of his explanation of why the elections were not held, see Appendix 1.

[2] *Department of State Bulletin*, Aug. 2, 1954 (immediately following the Geneva Accords of July 1954). During his CBS-TV appearance of Aug. 23, 1965, Secretary Rusk stated that while the United States did not sign the Geneva Accords, "General Bedell Smith, who was then Undersecretary of State, made a statement at the time which in effect embraced those agreements on behalf of the United States . . ."

[3] They are presumably the "tools" of the Soviet Union, China, or a more vague "world conspiracy." It is not certain that Mr. Rusk has relinquished this simple-minded view (in 1951 he regarded the Chinese Communist government as a "colonial Russian government, a Slavonic Manchukuo"), but its inadequacy is generally recognized by students of the Communist world. These matters are discussed further in Appendix 2 on "Independence."

had met nobody informed on the subject who did not agree that "possibly 80 per cent" of the Vietnamese people would have chosen Ho Chi Minh in a free election,[4] still attempted to organize a coalition to fight this successful nationalist revolution—in the interest of repelling "aggression" and maintaining an "independent" Vietnam.[5]

The ultimate product of the American coalition effort—the Bao Dai-Ngo Diem government set up in the Southern regrouping zone—could never have survived any reasonably free elections, such as those which were to take place in July 1956. In addition to President Eisenhower's estimate of an 80 per cent vote for Ho Chi Minh in 1954, columnist Joseph Alsop stated, after a trip through Vietnam in August 1954: "In the area I visited, the Communists have scored a whole series of political, organizational, military and one has to say it—moral triumphs.. . . What impressed me most, alas, was the moral fervor they had inspired among the non-Communist cadres and the strong support they had obtained from the peasantry."[6] Later, in March 1955, Alsop reported from Saigon that "If you ask the Americans here, they will tell you that outside of the feudal domains of the military and religious sects, anywhere from 50 to 90 per cent of the Southern Indochinese villages

---

[4] *Mandate For Change* (Garden City, N.Y., 1963), p. 372. In an address at the University of Pennsylvania on Jan. 26, 1966, Senator Wayne Morse stated that in 1954 U.S. intelligence services estimated an 80 per cent vote for Ho Chi Minh in the Southern regrouping zone (now South Vietnam).

[5] In view of the importance of the alleged "aggression" of North Vietnam in justifying current American intervention, it is of relevance that Eisenhower, Dulles, and Nixon all termed the Vietnamese struggle against the French a case of "aggression," despite the admittedly massive popular support for the Vietminh. Moreover, they came close to precipitating a war against the Vietminh and China, which were both alleged to be "aggressors" against the "independent" Indochina. The analogy to the present American intervention is a close one. See further Appendix 3, "Agression By Whom?", and the discussion of the premises of American diplomacy in 1953-54, in Chapter IV, pp. 35-36.

[6] *New York Herald Tribune*, Aug. 31, 1954.

are subject to Vietminh influence or control."[7] Leo Cherne, one
of the original promoters of the Diem "alternative," wrote in
Look magazine (January 25, 1955), referring to the elections he
fully expected to take place: "If elections were held today, the
overwhelming majority of Vietnamese would vote Communist.
. . . No more than 18 months remain for us to complete the
job of winning over the Vietnamese before they vote. What
can we do?"

Because such vivid handwriting was on the wall, the United
States was already addressing itself to the unsavory task of
blocking a legal self-determination that was obviously going to
unify Vietnam under Ho Chi Minh. Novelist Graham Greene
remarked in May 1955: "[Now] you will find no Vietnamese
who believes that the elections will ever be held. . . . No one
has the slightest doubt that Ho Chi Minh could agree to any
form of supervision without risk; his majority in the North
and in the South is assured. . . . In Hanoi they can afford to
keep the peace and wait."[8] Little wonder then that the United
States supported Diem in his defiance of the election proviso.
Despite the several different explanations by the U. S. State
Department on why the 1956 elections were never carried out,[9]
the story is plain to see: self-determination through any sort
of electoral plebiscite would have resulted in a sweeping Vietminh
victory.

From 1955 to the present, the dominant influence of the
United States has produced no free elections in South Vietnam.[10]

---

[7] Quoted by Ellen Hammer, *The Struggle for Indochina* (Stan-
ford, 1954), p. 36. Hammer herself observed that "some experts
believed that the Vietminh was stronger south of the 17th parallel
than it was in the North" (*ibid.*, p. 22).

[8] *New Republic*, May 9, 1955.

[9] See Appendix 1, "The Failure to Hold Elections in 1956."

[10] In an interview published in *Life* (Nov. 27, 1964), the U.S.
Deputy Ambassador to South Vietnam, U. Alexis Johnson, stated
that "During the whole period of their [South Vietnam's] colonial
administration, no independent political activity was permitted.
This was also true, from 1954 to 1963, during the Diem period."
What an admission to make when we have been engaging in mas-

There have been several elections with 98 per cent majorities (obtained by Diem even in areas entirely outside of government control), but in fact the degree of democracy in South Vietnam has declined under U. S. auspices. This has been primarily a consequence of the destruction by Diem of the centuries-old village councils, an important mechanism of local self-rule, and their replacement by Saigon-appointed administrators. The central government, under Diem and his military successors, has depended almost exclusively on the use of force to consolidate its internal power and has placed minimal reliance on political, social and economic reform.[11]

"By 1961," as John McDermott has pointed out in his extensive review of Vietnamese policy, "most of the countryside had gone to the Vietcong in spite of—or, more accurately, because of—the Agroville Program and its predecessors. . . . [Then came the even more drastic and disastrous Strategic Hamlet Program which forcibly relocated over 8 million rural inhabitants of South Vietnam in 1962 and 1963.] Thus, by a system of totalitarian controls, by a series of military expeditions against its own peasantry, and by the forced regroupment of almost the entire rural population did the Government of the Republic of Vietnam attempt to pacify the countryside.

"In a period of eight years, the entire social system of the

---

sive killing and destruction in the name of South Vietnamese "freedom"!

An eloquent Vietnamese response to the American rhetoric about "freedom" was made by a group of South Vietnamese Buddhists, Catholics, and intellectuals in July 1965:

"Liberty? For nine years under American patronage the people of South Vietnam have supported Diem's 'personalist' liberty in jail, in 'prosperity zones,' in strategic hamlets. They have had enough. The 'Free World'? This is perhaps an important reason for the Americans, and a cause for which Americans can die. But the population of South Vietnam is profoundly wary of the 'Free World.' For nearly 100 years this so-called Free World has brought Vietnam nothing but humiliation, servitude, exploitation, disasters, and wars." (*Viet-Report*, Nov.-Dec. 1965.)

[11] In 1955, well before the initiation of the really severe repressions of the Diem regime, the French correspondent Max Clos wrote: "Oddly enough, M. Diem has borrowed from his enemies what is most reprehensible in their methods: the denial of freedom

countryside was destroyed. . . . The regroupment schemes had convinced the peasantry that Vietcong propaganda was accurate. Diem was a puppet. . . . Because he was under the control of the Americans he was willing to raze the houses of the people, destroy the shrines of their ancestors, tear up sacred burial grounds, and force a helpless people into what a *Wall Street Journal* reporter called 'concentration camps'."[12]

With these developments, the "legitimacy" of the Saigon governments became even more dependent on support by the United States. When Washington became convinced that the Diem government had become a liability in fighting the war, its days were numbered. The criterion applied in judging the successor cliques has been their dedication to vigorous pursuit of military victory against the NLF. [13]

In his speech of July 28, 1965, President Johnson put the United States on record as favoring free elections "in the South, or throughout all Vietnam under international supervision." This was a substantial change in the American position, which had formerly been expressed in even vaguer generalities ("independence," "self-determination," "freedom"), and had tended

---

of opinion, the deification of the man who incarnates the regime and also the form of hypocrisy which attributes to the 'people's will' measures taken against those whom one considers as political opponents. . . . The Vietminh dictatorship is at least as odious as that of M. Diem. But it can show results in the political and economic fields." (*Le Monde*, Dec. 1, 1955, quoted in Donald Lancaster, *The Emancipation of French Indo-China*, Oxford, 1961, p. 399.)

For a description of the "series of man-hunts" launched by the Diem regime in 1957, which "became more frequent and more brutal" in 1958, and "very soon set the villagers against the regime", see Philippe Devillers, "The Struggle for Unification of Vietnam," *The China Quarterly*, Jan.-March, 1962, reprinted in Marvin E. Gettleman, ed., *Vietnam* (New York, 1965), pp. 222-225.

[12] "Profile of Vietnamese History (II)," *Viet-Report*, Aug.-Sept. 1965.

[13] This standard is fully met by General Ky, who has made neutralism a capital crime in South Vietnam, and who is dedicated to a fight to the bitter end (see Ch. V, note 19). That position follows logically from the fact that General Ky apparently is totally lacking in popular support in South Vietnam. Add to this the facts that

to avoid anything so specific as a commitment to free elections. For example, in a press conference held on February 25, 1965, it proved impossible to get Secretary Rusk to commit the United States to firm support of free elections, even under the most rigorous assumptions. The relevant exchange follows:

Reporter: "Mr. Secretary, were we satisfied that all supplies and infiltration from the North had been stopped, would the United States be content to solve the indigenous aspects, the civil war aspects, by free elections under international supervision in South Vietnam?"

Rusk: "Well, let's get to the first step first, and then if we get to that step, then we will have the luxury of indulging in the consideration of the second step."

Reporter: "What are our policies with regard to the indigenous aspects of a civil war? Could you enlighten us on this?"

Rusk: "Well, I think that the indigenous aspects of it could be brought to a conclusion very quickly, and that the South Vietnamese people could turn back to the problem of building their country and improving their constitutional system, elevating the economic standards of the country and get on with the modernization of the country which has been their purpose from the beginning."

Reporter: "But only by force, Mr. Secretary?"

Rusk: "I am not commenting on that. I think the pacification of the country would be easy if the external aggression were stopped."

Such refusal to contemplate anything but "pacification" is instructive. So is the fact that free elections were not mentioned in President Johnson's speech at Johns Hopkins on April 7. [14]

General Ky fought with the French Air Force against the Algerian Nationalists, and that in July 1965 he told a British reporter that his "only hero" was Adolf Hitler (*London Mirror*, July 4, 1965), and we have the portrait of the man Lyndon Johnson has embraced as the representative of the "free world" in Vietnam.

[14] In April 1965, Washington reporter I. F. Stone commented that "Over and over again I have put the question at press briefings— whether, if the rebels laid down their arms, we would be willing to abide by the results of free elections under international auspices. Neither on nor off the record have I been able to elicit a favorable response." (*I. F. Stone's Weekly*, April 19, 1965.)

It is true that Washington has moved toward verbal acceptance of free elections. But this adjustment was made only
after the expansion of American forces in Vietnam and widespread destruction and disorganization had greatly reduced the
feasibility of such elections. Moreover, the United States has
accepted the principle of free elections with so many reservations,
and it has exerted so little pressure for their effective implementation,[15] that this acceptance appears to have been employed
solely for public relations effect.

Among the reservations that sustain such scepticism, the
following are particularly important: First, the U. S. government has never committed itself to elections in which the NLF
could campaign and run its candidates freely. General Ky and
the military juntas have been adamantly opposed to this, and
so have key members of the Johnson administration. In an
interview in December 1965, Vice-President Humphrey indicated
that the NLF would not be permitted to participate in free elections since it is a "terrorist group" and "not a legitimate political
party."[16] This conception of free elections, which exclude "the
largest [political] force in the South" (according to Jean
Lacouture)[17] is obviously incompatible with a negotiated settlement of the Vietnamese conflict.

Second, in its replies to Senator Robert Kennedy's proposal,
in its commitments to General Ky, and in numerous other
public statements, the Johnson administration has taken a firm
stand against any broadly based, pre-election coalition government. Many informed observers consider such a coalition government to be an essential assurance of good faith (and means
of protection for the NLF against violations of the election agree-

---

[15] An understatement of the case. As we show presently, during
the spring and summer of 1966 the United States either supported
or acquiesced in actions by the Ky government that were wholly
incompatible with free elections.

[16] *Ramparts*, Feb. 1966. The Vice-President proved a good prophet.
On June 6, 1966, Senator Jacob Javits stated that the Ky government's electoral commission had decided to bar all those who "directly or indirectly work for Communists or neutralists" from the
elections scheduled for the fall of 1966. Senator Javits went on to
express fears that the U.S. government might support this decision,
thereby repudiating its commitment to "genuinely free elections."

ments)—thus a necessary prerequisite for organizing meaningful free elections in South Vietnam.

A third reservation, or ambiguity, in the U. S. acceptance of free elections centers in the apparent conflict of objectives pursued by Washington. Along with its expressed willingness to accept the results of free elections, the administration has also expressed a continuing determination to maintain an "independent (non-communist) South Vietnam." However, when these objectives came into conflict in 1955 and 1956, it was free elections (and self-determination) that were forced to give way. The real question is: would the United States now permit free elections if these seemed likely, or turned out to be, unfavorable?[18]

The plan developed in the spring of 1966 for free elections to be held in the summer was designed both to put an end to the "second" civil war and to reduce the pressure for a negotiated settlement of the larger conflict. (The Buddhists were split and "pacified" with the aid of the lure of possible political power to be obtained through an election; the American public, suddenly brought to wonder whether the people of South Vietnam "really want us there," was placated by a promised electoral test of Vietnamese opinion.) With the country in the midst of

---

(*Congressional Record*, June 6, 1966, p. 11801.) Since it was not until June 22 that the Ky government officially announced this decision, it is clear that Washington had ample notice of it, and thus time to do something about it, if this was considered desirable.

[17] *New York Review of Books*, March 3, 1966.

[18] There have been several indications from high U.S. sources that a Communist election victory would be *prima facie* evidence of an "unfree" election, or would by definition involve a continuation of "aggression."

According to Philippe Devillers, "When on August 12 [1965] I asked a high State Department functionary if the U.S. government would accept the results of free elections if the Communists won them, this was the exact reply: 'Your question is not realistic. If the elections are really free, they can't give victory to the Communists. For really free individuals can't vote Communist. If they give victory to the Communists it will be because the elections are not really free, and so we could hardly accept the results.'"

a savage war, with the countryside largely in the hands of the
NLF, and with a repressive military dictatorship holding power
in Saigon, free elections would be of dubious meaning under the
best imaginable electoral conditions. But the subsequent conversion of an unrealistic expedient into a cruel farce, with American acquiescence and support, has been revealing.

The following developments in regard to the forthcoming
(but already once postponed) elections are worthy of special
attention.

• The forcible suppression of the Buddhists in the late Spring
of 1966 permitted the military junta to weaken seriously the
only major, legal organized force in the cities of South Vietnam.
This set the stage for the ensuing emasculation of the electoral
process by the generals.[19]

• General Ky declared unilaterally that the Assembly to be
elected September 11, 1966 would have no legislative or execu-
tive powers. Its function is merely to write a constitution, after
which it will be dissolved, with General Ky retaining power
"until well into 1967."

• According to a decree law issued by the military junta
in June, to govern procedural rules for the prospective Assembly,
the junta is given a privileged position in the writing of the
constitution as well. Amendments which are proposed by the
junta can be rejected only by a two-thirds majority of the

(*Croissance des jeunes nations*, 1965, translated in *Viet-Report*,
Jan. 1966.)

More recently, Secretary Rusk has implied that a Communist electoral victory might be interpreted as continued "aggression."   (See
Arthur Krock, *New York Times*, Jan. 2, 1966.)

[19] According to Neil Sheehan, "The generals appear to regard the
elections and the constitution-making process as largely a method to
legitimize their own power and not as steps toward an eventual
civilian government." (*New York Times*, July 5, 1966.)

That this process is entirely compatible with American intentions in South Vietnam is reflected (among other evidence) in a
recent statement by C. L. Sulzberger, a strong supporter of administration policy. "Three months ago," he declared in the *New York
Times* of July 29, 1966, "an influential American in Saigon confided
that there wasn't any danger of 'losing' the promised national election in South Vietnam, adding: 'No hostile government will get in.
We'll see to that'."

Assembly. "Thus, if the junta can influence slightly more than one-third of the Deputies, it can virtually control the nature of the constitution."[20]

• In early May, General Ky announced that if a free election were won by Communists or neutralists, he would fight to prevent them from taking power. Secretary Rusk quickly claimed that General Ky had been misquoted. Ky thereupon repeated his statement. Secretary Rusk then lapsed into silence.

• On June 22, the electoral commission appointed by the junta proclaimed that neither Communists nor neutralists would be allowed to run for office, with the decision as to legitimacy resting solely with the Saigon government. This was the final step in the conversion of the elections into authoritarian comedy, and it occurred without any major reaction from the U. S. government (see note 16, above). It reveals with crystal clarity both the public relations function of the scheduled elections and the true nature of Washington's commitment to free elections (and freedom) in Vietnam.

Firepower and a prolonged "pacification" are clearly a safer route to maintaining an "independent" South Vietnam than really free elections—especially since it appears likely that the NLF would win an election victory. Some of the abundant evidence in support of this assertion is presented in Appendix 3; here we merely call attention to the following:

• The stream of statements from Washington, Saigon, and Honolulu, calling for a "social revolution" to win over the Vietnamese people, amounts to a continuing admission that the U. S.-supported government does not have the backing of the mass of the population.

Reports from Saigon published early in 1966 (*Washington Star,* January 14-15), pointed out, for example, that Ambassador Lodge "has repeatedly stressed that political remedies involved in 'true revolution' are basic preconditions to winning the war. Yet both Lodge and his top political aide, retired Maj. Gen. Edward Lansdale are known to have become increasingly discouraged. . . . They have encountered formidable opposition

---

[20] Sheehan, *loc. cit.*

from the land-owning urban middle class . . . [which] has no
intention of giving up its favored economic and political position.
Instead it seeks victory almost solely through military action
in an expanded war."

• That a significant portion of this alienated populace positively supports the NLF has been acknowledged by General Ky
himself, in his admission to James Reston "that the Communists
are closer to the people's yearnings for social justice and an
independent life than his own government." Ky later added
that his own government will not be able to compete politically
with the NLF "for some time."[21]

• The lesser appeal of General Ky than the NLF to the people
of South Vietnam is manifested in the profound difference in
fighting effort put forth by the Saigon and NLF soldiers. The
most striking of many testimonials to this difference is that of
U. S. Major Charles Beckwith at the hotly contested battle of
Pleime.

"Major Beckwith called the attacking troops [NLF and North
Vietnamese] 'the finest soldiers I have ever seen in the world
except Americans. I wish we could recruit them,' he said. 'I wish
I knew what they were drugging them with to make them fight
like that. They are highly motivated and highly dedicated.' "[22]

• The strength of popular support for the NLF is also evident
in its continued domination of the countryside, despite the im-
mense American military effort—a domination which can be
explained only by widespread peasant support of the NLF guerrillas. According to former Master Sergeant Donald Duncan,
decorated veteran of U. S. Special Forces in Vietnam, the growth
of the NLF in recent years "is not only impossible without popular
support, it actually requires an overwhelming mandate."[23]

• The fact that "Veteran American advisers [in Vietnam]

---

[21] *New York Times*, Sept. 1, 1965, and Jan. 15, 1966.

[22] *New York Times*, Oct. 28, 1965. On the lack of motivation of the
Saigon troops, see Charles Mohr, *New York Times*, Aug. 29, 1965
and Neil Sheehan, *New York Times*, May 13, 1966.

[23] " 'The Whole Thing Was a Lie'," *Ramparts*, Feb. 1966. The "terror" theory of NLF success, Duncan points out, is completely contrary
to both Special Forces doctrine and historical experience in guerrilla warfare. "South Vietnam," he states, "is a relatively small

see the American buildup as simply a bigger and better crutch to prop up a diseased government . . . If the shooting stopped tomorrow in Vietnam, the Communists could well win the goals for which they are fighting [via national elections], in the view of knowledgeable Americans here." [24]

The probable "unfavorable" outcome of free elections in South Vietnam is a commonplace in Washington as well. Senator Richard Russell stated over nationwide television on August 1, 1965, that "probably 75 per cent" of all South Vietnamese would vote for "Uncle Ho" if given the chance. In his Washington report of September 26, 1965, in the *Philadelphia Bulletin*, Robert Roth stated: "It has been said repeatedly that all the U.S. wants is an independent, freely elected government of South Vietnam, free of Communist aggression and terrorism. No one has figured out how to achieve this. It is reasonably certain that a free election will produce a Communist government in South Vietnam." [25]

It would appear, then, that if the Johnson administration is determined to do whatever is required to maintain an "independent" South Vietnam, there is no room for negotiation. It cannot firmly agree to free elections, since those elections would probably result in the exclusion of the United States from all of Vietnam. It is also difficult to imagine an administration which

---

country, dotted with thousands of small villages. In this very restricted area companies and battalions of Vietcong can maneuver and live under the very noses of government troops; but the people don't betray these movements, even though it is a relatively simple thing to pass the word. On the other hand, government troop movements are always reported."

On the question of "terror," Duncan declares that the truth is just the opposite of that generally conveyed to the American people; that is to say, the Saigon army troops regularly bring more terror to the rural population than the NLF forces.

[24] Ray Herndon, U.P.I., *Chicago Tribune*, Oct. 31, 1965.

[25] Roth appears to see no conflict between the notion that the Communists are aggressors and the fact that they would win a free election. It does not occur to him that the country intervening from 10,000 miles away to prevent self-determination might better deserve the designation aggressor.

invaded the Dominican Republic to prevent the return to power
of liberal non-communist Juan Bosch permitting major political
concessions to *genuine* Communists and fellow travellers.

Such concessions have never been admitted as subject to bargaining. This was indicated very clearly by Secretary Rusk in
December 1965. Max Frankel wrote in the *New York Times,*
December 8, 1965: "When asked . . . what the Communists
might salvage in negotiations for their many years of guerrilla
warfare, the Secretary added: 'It's not for me to say what the
Communists get out of it. We don't accept the view that the
burglar or robber is entitled to something just because he makes
the effort.' " (Ho Chi Minh, incidentally, has used the same
analogy to describe the role of the *United States* in Vietnam.)
Frankel goes on: "Mr. Rusk indicated that the Vietcong's political organization, the NLF, would not be given any political status
or influence in South Vietnam through negotiations."

The *New York Times* (December 12, 1965), had this to say
editorially about Secretary Rusk's position: "[He] gives the impression of placing more faith in military measures than in diplomacy. He has virtually ruled out compromise with the Communists in South Vietnam. 'Hanoi either leaves South Vietnam
alone or it does not' is a phrase that implies unconditional surrender rather than the unconditional negotiations President
Johnson has been urging." The *Times* editorial writer could not
bring himself to question the sincerity of President Johnson's own
urging of "unconditional discussions," but that a special meaning is attached to these words is evident. That meaning was
spelled out by Neil Sheehan in the *Times* on October 24, 1965:

"The Johnson Administration has, of course, repeatedly professed its willingness to go to the conference table at any time
and place for what are vaguely termed unconditional discussions. With considerably less fanfare, however, it has made
clear to Hanoi through neutral intermediaries and in the fine
print of its public pronouncements that it will not countenance a
Communist South Vietnam or the creation of any coalition regime in Saigon which *might* lead to a Communist seizure of
power.

"What Washington thus seems to mean by negotiations is a
conference at which Hanoi would agree to cease its activities in

the South, abandon its attempts to unify the country under Communist rule, and acquiesce in a permanent partition."

Sheehan's reporting of the administration position on negotiations was confirmed as accurate by the White House in October.[26] It was further confirmed and elaborated during the Fulbright hearings in February 1966, and in administration responses to Senator Robert Kennedy's suggestion that a coalition government including the NLF be established in South Vietnam.[27] In reporting recently on the "New Light on U.S. Policy" shed by the testimony of General Maxwell Taylor during the Fulbright hearings, Max Frankel pointed out that the goal of U.S. policy, that has "never wavered," is "to force the Communists to accept an independent and non-Communist South Vietnam."

"Many observers and diplomats here and abroad," Frankel reported, ". . . have misinterpreted the Administration's offer to negotiate as an offer to compromise with the Vietcong in South Vietnam. General Taylor's testimony should have made it clear that such a compromise is not anticipated here . . .

"[The Administration] has offered to consider the Vietcong's 'views' in negotiations and even to let the Vietcong sit in the delegation of North Vietnam, whose agents it says they are. Washington's purpose at such negotiations would be to ratify the end of the Communist threat to South Vietnam and not to compromise on the basis of the existing military balance.

"As General Taylor reiterated, the Administration believes the Communists have not been hurt sufficiently on the battlefield to enter into the kind of negotiations [sic] that have been offered. Privately, officials here agree with this presumed Communist assessment. They believe the Communists would now negotiate or give up only if they were prepared to honor the potential force that the U.S. can bring to bear." [28]

---

[26] *I. F. Stone's Weekly*, Nov. 22, 1965.

[27] In his comments on administration responses to Senator Kennedy, Arthur Krock observed that they added up to a demand for "unconditional surrender" by the NLF and "substantially promote the principal argument of Hanoi and of Peking for refusing to negotiate." (*New York Times*, Feb. 27, 1966.)

[28] *New York Times*, Feb. 18, 1966. For similar testimony that U.S. objectives necessarily require *de facto* surrender by North Vietnam

It will be noted that "negotiation" and the enemy's "giving up" are used as synonyms. Frankel does not call attention to the deceptiveness of this use of words, but it appears that "negotiation" and "unconditional discussions" have been employed by the Johnson administration both to manipulate public opinion and to balk any real chances of settlement. Washington's offers to "negotiate," i.e., accept surrender, carry their own built-in defenses against any meaningful diplomatic exchanges.[29]

It is also worth noting that the political feasibility of concessions (and thus *real* negotiations) has diminished in proportion to the increases in our commitment in Vietnam, and as a consequence of the war fever that the Johnson policy itself has generated in the United States. The sacrifices of lives could hardly be justified by a negotiated settlement which might have been attained through U Thant's efforts in 1964, and which the American right-wing would immediately label "sell-out." Thus Washington's goal continues to be an "independent" South Vietnam. However, since an "independent" South Vietnam cannot be gained through either free elections or negotiations that recognize the true distribution of power and popular support in that country, achievement of this goal requires forcibly imposing upon the Vietnamese people a minority government acceptable to the United States. This is aggression of the classic variety.

---

and the NLF, see Max Frankel, *New York Times*, Feb. 12, 1966, and Richard Eder, *New York Times*, Feb. 14, 1966.

[29] In the *New York Times*, Dec. 2, 1965, Secretary Rusk was reported as saying that the United States has been engaged in weekly inquiries directed to Hanoi through intermediaries, to ask whether a halt in the bombings would lead to "negotiations." It should be obvious at this juncture how one must interpret this kind of statement. And it should also be clear that this Orwellian use of "negotiations" is well suited to the public relations needs of a policy aimed at military victory.

III

THE LOGIC OF ESCALATION

Settlement of the war by negotiation would require political concessions reflecting the loss of the civil war in South Vietnam by the American-sustained (but Vietnamese-rejected) Saigon regimes. As we have observed, such a settlement would be intolerable to the Johnson administration.

The strategic purpose of escalation is, therefore, to do what has to be done militarily to prevent such political concessions. In the "tough minded" logic of geopolitics, it is deemed "workable" to achieve these goals simply by making our determination to win "credible." The enemy must know that we have enough military power actually to exterminate the population of Vietnam. If we steadily raise the level of escalation, presumably the NLF and North Vietnam will eventually recognize that permitting a government of our own choosing ("independent") is preferable to something approaching genocide.[1] Moreover, if we kill enough members of the NLF, as well as a sufficient number of its supporters in the villages "suspected of aiding the Vietcong," we might be able, it is thought, to reduce opposition to an "independent" government to manageable levels. As McGeorge Bundy indicated in his appearance on *Meet the Press* in the spring of 1965, this will require "stamina" on our part. Obviously, if the enemy foolishly refuses to surrender and we are obligated to escalate to the point of actual genocide, this is hardly our responsibility—we announced in advance that we would do what had to be done to maintain an "independent and free Vietnam."

So far this theory has worked out badly. Not only has Hanoi shown no signs of surrender, it has even had the audacity and wickedness to do a little escalating of its own. And the escalation of the war has increasingly had the disastrous effect of mak-

---

[1] See Appendix 4, "Genocide in Vietnam?"

31

ing the war a conflict between the United States and the Vietnamese people.[2] The massive American intervention, the almost
complete take-over of the fighting by U.S. personnel,[3] the rising
levels of death and devastation meted out by these forces, have
strengthened the nationalistic appeal of the NLF in South Vietnam. That appeal is surely not weakened by the fact that all
but one of the Saigon generals, including General Ky himself,
fought with the French in the pre-1954 struggle to free Indochina
from colonial status. The base of the Saigon junta government
has shrunk to a point of tragi-comical insignificance; and with
this development the United States has been stripped of a
credible alternative in South Vietnam.[4] The NLF gains recruits,
grows despite severe casualties, and fights well. The Saigon government troops keep on deserting at an increasing rate,[5] and they

---

[2] This has frequently been commented upon in India, Japan, and
the rest of Asia, and it has awakened consciences in the United
States as well. On Dec. 3, 1965, the General Board of the National
Council of Churches warned that "no conceivable victory [in Viet-
nam] can compensate for the distrust and hatred that is being generated each day throughout much of the world because we are seen
as a predominantly white nation using our overwhelming military
strength to kill more and more Asians."

[3] By mid-1966 this take-over was beginning to produce its own
irrefutable statistics. On June 17, 1966, U.P.I. reported (*Philadelphia Inquirer*) that American combat casualties had exceeded South
Vietnamese, for the sixth consecutive week.

[4] In the July 1965 statement by a group of South Vietnamese (see
Ch. II, note 10), this point was made with eloquence:
"What is the present situation in South Vietnam? There are two
realities and only two: the United States and the National Liberation Front. The nationalist government, which during the time of
Diem was still able to preserve a shadow of reality, is losing even
this shadow and has become, in the words of Pascal, 'a nothing between two infinities.'
"The fundamental flaw of American policy is that the more mas-
sively and directly it intervenes in this war, the more it destroys
the reality of the government on whose behalf it is intervening.
And in consequence, the more it destroys the legitimacy of its
intervention."

[5] See the A.P. dispatch from Saigon, *Washington Star*, Nov. 22,
1965, and Neil Sheehan, " '65 Desertions Up in Saigon Forces," *New
York Times*, Feb. 24, 1966. Desertions in 1966 have run 20 per cent
above the level reported by Sheehan; A.P., Aug. 29, 1966.

often fight badly—apparently not recognizing that the United States is helping them defend their "freedom and independence."

Since further escalation will almost certainly have effects in the same perverse direction, extraordinary stamina will be imperative. Our options are still what they were in the fall of 1964: a costly and drawn-out process of frightful slaughter and attempted conquest (with possible escalation beyond Vietnam into China), or political concessions to the NLF, which our own policies have helped to consolidate as the most significant (although not the only) indigenous political power in South Vietnam. As we have pointed out, the Johnson administration has explicitly rejected admission of the NLF to membership in a coalition government. The official theory, clung to with bulldog-like tenacity, is that the NLF is a tool of Hanoi, and that Hanoi can call off its "aggression" if it so desires.[6] The NLF is not acknowledged to have any substantial, long term support in South Vietnam.[7] As long as a governmental role for the NLF is not a negotiable matter for the United States, this country's policy must be regarded as one of insistence on surrender by the enemy, and one in which an appeal for "negotiations" and "unconditional discussions" is merely a mechanism for manipulating public opinion.

One final point must be added on the logic of military escala-

---

[6] This theory is not necessarily *believed* in Washington. In a discussion of official thinking on negotiations, Max Frankel said that one difficulty attributed to negotiations with China or North Vietnam is that "they could not persuade the Vietcong to lay down their arms without assuring them a dominant position in future Saigon governments—the equivalent, in Washington's eyes, of defeat." ("Washington Still Rules Out Any Vietnam Negotiations," *New York Times,* Feb. 18, 1965.) More recently, Frankel stated that "Even more perplexing to officials here [Washington] is their inability to judge the degree of Hanoi's influence over the Vietcong. They have judged that influence to be considerable in military terms, but they do not know whether North Vietnam could negotiate an end to hostilities even if it wanted to." (*New York Times,* Jan. 1, 1966.) The advantage of the official theory is that by denying the *civil* aspect of the conflict and insisting on its being external aggression, no limit is placed on the degree of violence that can be applied to prevent loss of the *civil* war.

[7] See Appendix 3 for a discussion of relative degrees of support for the NLF and for the U.S.-supported junta governments of Saigon.

tion. While the process of escalation has had the strategic aims and effects just discussed, it has also been employed for tactical purposes as well. As is evident in subsequent chapters, escalation of the war has been used systematically by Washington as a means of putting an end to any diplomatic moves, or domestic or foreign pressures, that seriously threaten to lead to a negotiated settlement of the conflict in Vietnam.[8] These pressures have resulted from increasing domestic dissatisfaction, from political unrest and the surfacing of neutralist sentiments in South Vietnam, and from peace efforts initiated by the NLF, by North Vietnam, or by third parties. When the pressures have become substantial, Washington has invariably initiated a peace gesture as part of its public relations strategy. This in turn, having served its purpose, has usually been brought to a decisive end by renewed escalation.

---

[8] This is the main theme of a recently published and well-documented monograph, *The Politics of Escalation. A study of United States Responses to Pressures for a Political Settlement of the Vietnam War: November 1963-January 1966*, by Franz Schurmann, Peter Scott, and Reginald Zelnick of the University of California, Berkeley.

IV

THE DIPLOMACY OF A "WIN POLICY" (I)

The policy of the United States toward negotiations with the
Vietminh, the NLF, and North Vietnam, a policy maintained without interruption since 1953, has been one of total unwillingness
to pursue a diplomatic solution of outstanding issues.

During the period immediately preceding the Geneva Accords
of 1954, the weight of American power was thrown consistently
against a negotiated settlement, in favor of continuing the fighting and expanding it by means of a coalition effort. In February
1954, for example, the British Ambassador was told at the State
Department "that the U.S. Government were perturbed by the
fact that the French were aiming not to win the war, but to get
into a position from which they could negotiate."[1] On April 4,
1954, President Eisenhower sent Winston Churchill a personal
note in which he emphasized that "there was no negotiated solution of the Indo-China problem" and that what was required was
concerted action against Communist aggression. This was accompanied by a State Department proposal for joint action
against the aggression committed by China by its intervention in
the Indochina war.[2] According to the *London Times* of April
9, 1954, "Dulles with the President's support . . . has suggested
that a Communist victory, *even if achieved with Vietnam forces
alone*, is not to be tolerated."

The U.S. effort to continue and expand the war foundered in
1954, largely as a result of opposition by the British government
(and some American generals). This failure was followed by an

---

[1] Anthony Eden, *Full Circle* (London, 1960), p. 100.

[2] This policy was proposed despite the fact that, as Eisenhower
himself acknowledges in his memoirs, "there was no incontrover-
tible evidence of overt Red Chinese participation in the Indochinese
conflict." (*Mandate for Change*, p. 340.) In fact, as Eden notes,
"The Americans had put in nine times more supplies of materials
than the Chinese. . . ." (*Op. cit.*, pp. 126-27.)

unremitting effort to sabotage the Geneva Conference "by procedural and other steps hoping that Eden's sensitive diplomatic gambit would be disturbed thereby and that Communist China and the Vietminh would, by intransigence, help Dulles' game. These obstructions were obvious to the Conference participants. . . . The final and last obstructive act of the American Delegation, was, of course, their refusal to sign any of the Agreements or the Final Declaration." [3] Sir Anthony Eden states in his autobiography that, "As I reported to London at the time, *the Americans seemed clearly apprehensive of reaching any agreement, however innocuous*, with the Communists." [4]

In the succeeding years, during which American power displaced the French in South Vietnam, the paralyzing effects of U.S. anti-Communism on diplomacy became decisive. "At no time after Geneva, between 1954 and 1959-60," according to Victor Bator, "was the slightest endeavour made to use diplomacy in order to turn the confrontation of the Free World with the Communist Powers in Indochina into a state of tolerable coexistence. The processes of diplomacy were not only ignored but explicitly rejected. Vice President Nixon summed up the American position for the future of Indochina: 'It is impossible to lay down arms until victory is completely won!' " [5]

---

[3] Victor Bator, *Vietnam: A Diplomatic Tragedy* (Dobbs Ferry, N.Y., 1965), pp. 93, 95.

[4] Eden, *Full Circle*, pp. 142-3. Donald Lancaster observed that ". . . whereas the French and British delegates [to Geneva] were most anxious to reach a settlement, Dulles was precluded both by his personal convictions and by the attitude of Congress from taking part in negotiations which were likely to result in an armistice involving concessions to Asian Communists." (*Op. cit.*, pp. 315-16, reprinted in Gettleman, *Vietnam*, p. 121.)

[5] Bator, *Vietnam*, p. 224. In reviewing Bator's book, Bernard Fall remarks on this passage: "That point needs to be rammed home with force today when it is being deplored *urbi et orbi* that the Communists are not responding to American offers to negotiate: There is a fairly solid record that, particularly in 1956-58, when they experienced serious economic troubles, the Hanoi leaders were willing to negotiate extensive 'de facto' economic and cultural agreements with South Vietnam which might well have given them a stake in not upsetting a mutually profitable status quo. They

This incapacity for diplomacy has continued through the Kennedy and Johnson administrations. The only acceptable solution to an obviously civil war, and a deteriorating military and political situation, appears to be continued support for a military victory over the NLF. When asked about U.S. policy toward any new government in South Vietnam, President Kennedy replied: "If it helps win the war we support [it]. What interferes with the war effort we oppose."[6] This stand not only precluded negotiations, it also tended to undermine the sporadic efforts at encouraging social and economic reform (they "rocked the boat") and led to ready acquiescence in authoritarian government.

It is interesting to note that in a recent enumeration by the State Department of "Negotiation Attempts on Vietnam"[7] made by the United States since 1960, there is no mention of even a token move to settle the Vietnamese war by diplomacy at any time before the escalation of February 1965. The omission reflects the fact that throughout 1963 and 1964 nearly all concerned parties *except* the United States were trying to initiate negotiations.

In this period a series of proposals for conferences and bases of settlement were made by General de Gaulle, by Ho Chi Minh, and by U Thant. In August 1963, and again in July 1964, de Gaulle made major pleas for the unification and neutralization of Vietnam. But, as Jack Raymond reported in the *New York Times* on August 23, 1964, "The administration has consistently turned away proposals for neutralization as an outcome of the hostilities in South Vietnam. President De Gaulle of France, in his proposals for such a settlement, has been rebuffed repeatedly at the White House and the State Department." In fact, Washington was not only turning away proposals for neutralization; it was explicitly rejecting the very idea of a negotiated settlement. In his press conference of July 24, 1964, one day after a de Gaulle neutralization proposal, President Johnson

---

were either totally ignored, or turned down by Diem with outright insults, deluded as he was about his own strength." (*New Republic*, July 10, 1965.)

[6] Press conference, *New York Times*, Sept. 13, 1963.

[7] State Department, Bureau of Public Affairs, 4/34b-1165BT.

stated: "We do not believe in conferences called to ratify terror, so our policy is unchanged."

A de Gaulle-type neutralization idea was widely reported to be favored by Ho Chi Minh in 1963 and 1964. Eastern European diplomats claimed that Ho wished to escape from the arena of the Sino-Soviet conflict and from the "suffocating" pressure of China (based on North Vietnamese dependence on China for rice and other foods). To other observers "Ho Chi Minh is potentially a Titoist who would wrench North Vietnam loose if the major powers gave him a chance."[8] In an article based on "unimpeachable U.N. sources," the U.N. correspondent of the *Manchester Guardian,* Hella Pick, reported that in the transition period following the overthrow of Ngo Dinh Diem in November 1963, Ho Chi Minh approached the U.S. government in an effort to initiate talks and possibly to arrive at a settlement. His effort did not even elicit a response from the United States.[9] Furthermore, at the same time the NLF in South Vietnam scaled down its operations and announced its readiness to negotiate an end to the insurrection. This and all other NLF efforts were ignored by the United States and the Saigon generals.[10]

A further effort at diplomacy occurred in the summer of 1964, when U Thant proposed a reconvening of a Geneva Conference for the purpose of negotiating an end to the fighting in Vietnam. This effort was supported by the Soviet Union, France, and

------

[8] M. S. Handler, "Neutral Vietnam Held North's Aim," *New York Times,* Nov. 5, 1963, and Tad Szulc, "Peking and Hanoi Said to Differ on Approach to Crisis in Saigon," *New York Times,* Aug. 30, 1963. In 1962 the expert French reporter on Vietnam, Jean Lacouture, wrote that "The Ho Chi Minh group is very wary of China. It emphasizes the reunification of the two Vietnams. It leans toward a Vietnamese 'nationalist' policy . . . toward reconstructing, for the benefit of Hanoi, what was once Indochina. This project is most disquieting to Peking." (*New Republic,* May 21, 1962.) Incapable of exploiting such a division, American anti-Communism must instead push Hanoi into greater dependence on China.

[9] Hella Pick, "Hanoi Feelers Were Rebuffed by Washington," *Manchester Guardian Weekly,* Aug. 12, 1965.

[10] These NLF offers were made on several occasions from November 1963 through January 1964. Jean Lacouture, *Vietnam Between Two Truces* (English translation; New York, 1966), pp. 169-171.

China. The United States, however, opposed the reconvening of either the 1954 or 1962 conferences. Its opposition reportedly resulted from the fact that "it [the U. S. government] believes the issue involved is to carry out existing agreements, using existing machinery. United States sources add that in view of repeated violations of the existing agreements, there is no point in negotiating new ones." [11] Apart from the transparent weakness of this excuse (only partially a result of the fact that the U.S. and Saigon governments have been the principal violators of the Geneva Accords),[12] it represents only another incident in the long line of American refusals to negotiate a Vietnamese settlement.

Washington's unwillingness to engage in peaceful dialogue throughout the summer of 1964 was emphasized by the Gulf of Tonkin incident, which grew out of events that occurred within one week after the diplomatic efforts just mentioned. On August 2nd and August 4th, North Vietnamese torpedo boats allegedly attacked American warships operating in the Gulf. Later, these ships were revealed to have been not only in close proximity to South Vietnamese naval vessels engaged in shelling two islands off the North Vietnamese coast, they were also "on an electronic surveillance mission, monitoring radar defenses and radio communications in North Vietnam" (John Finney, *New York Times*, September 25, 1964). In quick retaliation for this "unprovoked aggression" (in the words of President Johnson), the United States carried out its first major aerial bombardment of North Vietnam.

This U.S. attack cannot reasonably be regarded as a simple, isolated act of reprisal. On the contrary, the evidence now available suggests that the torpedo boat attack may never have taken place, and that the incident was staged, either in whole or in part, to provide a convenient excuse for attacking North Vietnam.[12A] But whether or not this episode was manufactured,

---

[11] "Thant Proposes Vietnam Parley to End Fighting," *New York Times*, July 9, 1964.

[12] See the International Control Commission *Reports* in Gettleman, *Vietnam*, pp. 160-90, and Appendix 1, below.

[12A] Shortly after the incident, the Pentagon clamped a tight veil of secrecy over the whole affair and forbade all U.S. Navy per-the nature and scale of the administration's response conveyed a distinct message to the parties actively searching for a basis of settlement of the growing crisis in Vietnam. The United States was demonstrating in no uncertain terms, and in a language soon to become familiar, its distaste for diplomacy.

The same can, of course, be said of official American reaction to the two U Thant-Hanoi approaches for discussions and negotiations in the fall of 1964. These were turned down not because the antennae of the Secretary of State detected "insincerity" on the part of North Vietnam (as clear an example of *ex post facto* fabrication as one could expect to find), but because the United States was adhering to its policy of complete refusal to attempt to negotiate a settlement.

Official U.S. denials of any interest in third-party mediation were issued weekly through the early months of 1965. U Thant's plan to convene a multi-national conference on Indochina was promptly rejected by the State Department on February 24, despite pressures from both Britain and France. Two weeks after the February 7 escalation of the war into the North, Hanoi notified the Secretary-General that it was "receptive to his suggestion for informal negotiations on the Vietnam situation." [13] On the same day, the *Times* reported Rusk's reply that North Vietnam "must indicate a willingness to end its aggression" before the United States would consider negotiations, and noted that the Secretary "refused to specify what indications would be acceptable to the administration." Two days later the State Department issued its White Paper charging massive intervention by North Vietnam, and soon thereafter Washington announced its continuing policy of air attacks on the North.

The only departure from this tradition in more recent develop-

---

sonnel involved in it to discuss it in any way. See however, *Ramparts*, June 1966, p. 14; *I .F. Stone's Bi-Weekly*, August 24, 1964; *The Politics of Escalation*, pp. 15-22; Andrew Kopkind, in the *New Statesman*, July 22, 1966; and James Reston's column in the *New York Times* of October 2, 1964, in which he reports that U.S. government officials were "talking casually about how easy it would be to 'provoke an incident' in the Gulf of Tonkin that would justify an attack on North Vietnam . . ."

[13] *New York Times*, Feb. 26, 1965.

ments, to which we now turn, is the *pretended* interest in negotiations.

Suddenly, in a brief address delivered by the President on March 25, the Johnson administration made its verbal adjustment: "As I have said in every part of the Union, I am ready to go anywhere at any time, and meet with anyone whenever there is promise of progress toward an honorable peace." After offering his package of economic aid to the entire Southeast Asian region, he continued: "We have said many times . . . that we seek no more than a return to the essentials of the agreements of 1954." Shortly thereafter a *Times* correspondent reported from Moscow that "North Vietnamese officials indicated that their government might be willing to agree to a new Geneva Conference on Indochina." [14] Neither President Johnson nor the State Department made any response to this expression of interest.

At Johns Hopkins on April 7 another audience was favored with a restatement of the line, only this time Mr. Johnson went further in offering "unconditional discussions with any government." It came at a time when domestic and foreign criticism of American policy had reached a clamorous volume, and bitter accusations were being hurled at the United States from many corners of the globe. Some response was inescapable. The President's speech was greeted at home and abroad with an almost audible sigh of relief. It again became possible for many American liberals, uncomfortable in opposition to a "liberal" Democrat in the White House, to flock back under the more cozy "consensus" tent of the President. As Senator Wayne Morse pointed out the next day: "Now, so the argument goes, we can say that we have offered to negotiate a peace and if the offer is not accepted, it is the fault of someone else, not the United States." But this was all contingent on avoiding a close look at the details of Mr. Johnson's speech, its context, and its follow-up.

The April 7th speech did not propose "negotiations". It merely announced a willingness to engage in "discussions". This usage was not inadvertent. According to Washington reporter I. F.

---

[14] *New York Times*, April 1, 1965.

Stone in his *Weekly* of April 19, "just before the speech was delivered, unnameable administration spokesmen were assuring the
foreign press and the *hoi polloi* of our own, though not for at-
tribution, that the speech was a turn toward peace talks. But at
private sessions later for hard-line U. S. commentators, emphasis
was placed on the belligerent passages and on a tricky distinction between 'discussions' and 'negotiations.' Only the former,
it was explained, were to be without preconditions."

This distinction, and the real pre-conditions, were spelled out
to the enemy in a leaflet published by the South Vietnamese
government on April 11, 1965, and scattered by U.S. planes over
North Vietnam.[15] The leaflet indicated that the NLF would not
be permitted to participate in any negotiations and that negotiations would not take place until after "preconditions . . . laid
out by the Republic of Vietnam during eventual preliminary
talks will have been accepted and carried out." The "preconditions" included the "previous withdrawal of the Vietcong units
and political cadres."

The American people were not told about the aforementioned
leaflet, but Henry Cabot Lodge spoke rather frankly when he
appeared on the *Meet the Press* television program on May 23rd.
"Negotiations," he declared, would be disastrous, "the equivalent
of turning South Vietnam over to the wolves." However, "if
they accepted our invitation to 'discuss' and it meant that they
had a change of heart, then of course it would be worth doing."
In other words, concessions to the NLF would be required by
meaningful negotiations; "discussions" committed us to nothing
and would be worthwhile as a mechanism whereby the NLF and
Hanoi could communicate their willingness to surrender.

The meaning of the Johns Hopkins speech is also revealed by
its refusal to recognize the existence of the NLF as a power entity
in South Vietnam. While admitting that "some of the people
of South Vietnam are participating in attacks on their own government," the President described support from Hanoi as "the
heartbeat of the war." With this rhetoric, a civil war was turned

---

[15] This leaflet was obtained from the U.S. Information Agency in
Saigon by the authors of the publication of the American Friends
Service Committee, *Peace in Vietnam: A New Approach to South-
east Asia* (New York, 1966), pp. 53-54.

into "aggression," although support from Washington was even more obviously the "heartbeat" of the military endeavors of the Saigon governments. With still fuzzier rhetoric "the deepening shadow of Communist China" was brought in to establish "a wider pattern of aggressive purpose." Thus a civil war in Vietnam, with the United States the only non-Vietnamese interventionist, was made to appear a Chinese responsibility by very indirect proxy.[16]

It should also be noted that the unlimited "discussions" offered by President Johnson were strictly confined to governments—that is, to anybody but the South Vietnamese parties with whom we were fighting. This is analogous to the behavior of the French in 1953-1954, when they continued to regard the Vietminh as an agent of China until they were forced to conclude that real negotiations were necessary. As Senator Morse said in his speech of April 8th: "We shall not have any real negotiations until we talk to the people who are fighting, *and we will not have a genuine offer to negotiate from the White House until the offer is directed to the people we are fighting and not to the shadows behind them."*

The Johnson speech of April 7th was also extremely vague as to possible terms of settlement of the war. Although reference

---

[16] Mr. Shinichi Matsumoto, the former Japanese Ambassador to Great Britain, who was sent by Premier Sato to survey the situation in Vietnam, remarked with irony: "It seems that the basic thinking of the United States is that Communist China or the Soviet Union is connected with North Vietnam and the Vietcong in a sort of parent-child-grandchild relationship. . . . However, there is no one who can define clearly the true character of the Vietcong. Even the people of Saigon . . . [estimate the Communists in the Vietcong to be] at the most, 30 per cent. . . . In Vietnam I often heard it said that the Vietcong is a nationalist movement. This means the Vietcong will not give up resistance until they have achieved their objectives."

It is also interesting that Mr. Matsumoto, who visited Vietnam just before President Johnson's April 7th speech, was impressed by the militaristic sentiment among the Americans there: "I heard not a word about peace from the United States side in Vietnam. . . . At any rate, I learned in Vietnam that both the U.S. State Department and the Defense Department have strong opinions. There is no possibility of the United States first bringing about talk of peace." (*New York Times*, April 7, 1965.)

was made to the desire that the people of South Vietnam be "allowed to guide their own country in their own way," no proposals were put forward even of a general character for free elections, or for a return to the Geneva Agreements. Our objective was stated to be the "independence of South Vietnam," undefined, but in a context strongly suggesting the Orwellian conception of "independence" described earlier. Left unconsidered, of course, was the possibility that in "guiding their own country in their own way" the people of South Vietnam might choose not to be "independent."

Significantly, no *deed*, such as a de-escalation of military activity, accompanied President Johnson's offer of "discussions." On the contrary, the April 7th speech was preceded by a decision to increase the American commitment in Vietnam; [17] and it was followed by a sharp increase in the number of U.S. troops in South Vietnam and a major intensification of air raids against the North. [18]

The North Vietnamese were quick to denounce the April 7th speech as "deceitful," and the Chinese claimed (accurately) that Mr. Johnson was in effect asking the NLF to "surrender unconditionally." Nevertheless, despite recognizing the basically public relations character of the speech, North Vietnam did make a counter-offer in the form of its own "four-point proposals" on the very next day. These four points were: (1) recognition of Vietnamese independence, unity and territorial integrity, whose primary requirement is the withdrawal of U.S. troops and weapons and the abolition of all foreign bases in Vienam; (2) observance of the 1954 Geneva Accords, forbidding the presence of foreign troops, pending reunification; (3) settlement of South Vietnam's internal affairs by the South Vietnamese, in accordance with the program of the NLF, without foreign interference; (4) reunification of Vietnam by peaceful means without foreign interference.

---

[17] This planned expansion was decided upon on April 2, according to the *New York Times* of April 3, 1965.

[18] In his message to Congress on May 4, President Johnson pointed out that sorties against North Vietnam increased from 160 in February to 1,500 in April. (*New York Times*, May 5, 1965.)

While containing some obviously ambiguous and debatable provisions, the Hanoi program essentially called for a return to the Geneva Accords of 1954. It was, in addition, much more specific than President Johnson's speech.

For some months after their introduction, the four points were subject to considerable misunderstanding, to which the Johnson administration contributed. On June 23rd Secretary Rusk said that "so far as we can determine" Hanoi will not negotiate unless U.S. forces are withdrawn *in advance.*[19] Two months later, when the administration line changed briefly, Max Frankel stated in the *New York Times* of August 25 that Hanoi's four point proposal "has been widely misinterpreted as a set of 'preconditions' for negotiations. Actually, the four points were followed by the statement that, if they were accepted as a 'basis' for a settlement, North Vietnam would find it possible to 'consider' the reconvening of an international conference."

In fact, although Hanoi and the NLF have made occasional statements indicating that total and immediate withdrawal of U.S. troops is a precondition for any talks, neither the NLF five point declaration of March 22, 1965 nor the four points of North Vietnam stipulated the prior withdrawal of American troops as a precondition. Moreover, flexibility about the timing of outside troop withdrawal has been suggested to Western visitors to Hanoi, and to others, on a number of occasions.[20]

Even the third point, often cited as the key obstacle to nego-

---

[19] Max Frankel, *New York Times*, June 24, 1965.

[20] This was the impression of Sanford Gottlieb of the Sane Nuclear Policy Committee, after talks with North Vietnamese and NLF officials during the Summer of 1965 in Paris and Algiers (*Sane World*, Sept. 1965). Lord Fenner Brockway of Great Britain reached the same conclusion after his August 1965 talks in Moscow with North Vietnamese and NLF officials: "[The North Vietnamese government] never insisted that all the American troops should be withdrawn before talks for a cease-fire took place or before negotiations" (*London Tribune*, Sept. 10, 1965).

For similar testimony, see Georges Chaffard, *L'Express*, April 12, 1965 (translated in *Viet-Report*, July 1965); Drew Pearson, *Philadelphia Bulletin*, Nov. 18, 1965; Bernard Fall, in New York Times, Dec. 12, 1965; Jacques Decornoy, *Le Monde*, Jan. 20-26, 1966; Seymour Topping and Robert Kleiman, *New York Times*, Feb. 6 and Feb. 14, 1966; and Drew Middleton, *New York Times*, Feb. 18, 1966.

tiations, is not simply a call for turning over South Vietnam to
the NLF. As the *New York Times* pointed out editorially on
January 9, 1966:

"Actually, Hanoi's Point Three is deliberately ambiguous. It
states: 'The internal affairs of South Vietnam must be settled by
its people, in accordance with the program of the National Liberation Front, without foreign intervention.'

"The two commas which Hanoi uses in this sentence—and
Peking usually omits—permit Point Three to be interpreted
liberally to mean: 'As stated in the program of the NLF, the internal affairs of South Vietnam must be settled by its people
without intervention.' . . . Negotiations can be blocked, but they
cannot be advanced by American insistence that North Vietnam
go further than at present in clarifying an ambiguity that Hanoi
evidently requires in order to dissemble its differences with
Peking."

In short, the Hanoi reply was one that could have begun a
dialogue, counter-proposals, and thus negotiations—if the United
States had really been interested. It was not, and the Hanoi
response was dismissed as totally unacceptable.

In a most illuminating turnabout in August, Messrs. Bundy,
Rusk, and Goldberg revived the Hanoi proposals of April 8th and
considered them point by point, on a CBS television panel.
According to Max Frankel, in his August 25th commentary on
this program, *"Officials here thought at the time* [i.e., in April]
*that many parts of the proposals were acceptable and that others
could be refined to become acceptable.* But it was not until July
28th that President Johnson offered publicly to discuss North
Vietnam's proposals, among others." This extraordinary statement confirms that in April the United States rejected out of
hand a Hanoi response that administration officials deemed a
reasonable basis for discussion. In other words, Hanoi success-
fully called the bluff of the Johnson administration in April, and
the administration refused to "discuss" (much less negotiate) a
proposal in part "acceptable" and in part needing "refinement."
Despite such evidence, President Johnson has continued to repeat

Middleton reported that in the fall of 1965 "a senior member of
President Johnson's administration" said that Hanoi was known to
be flexible on the matter of U.S. troop withdrawal.

piously, and practically without challenge, that the United States has been earnestly seeking negotiations, but has been unable to elicit any response from North Vietnam.

Only once before December 1965 did Washington briefly de-escalate the war. During the five day period May 13 to May 17 air attacks on North Vietnam were partially suspended.[21] Although this episode has been used effectively for advertising the intransigence of the enemy, at that time it was barely pretended to be a serious effort to bring about negotiations; it was meant to confound the administration's critics by *proving* Hanoi's disinterest. The purpose of the suspension was reported to be "to demonstrate that the Communist governments were not interested in negotiations . . . [and] to convince its critics at home and abroad that North Vietnam and China were preventing negotiations, not the United States." [22]

A number of persons—including Canadian Prime Minister Lester Pearson, the editors of the *New York Times,* and Senator J. W. Fulbright—had suggested that a temporary halt in the bombings might be a constructive move that would better test the enemy's desire to negotiate. The very caution of these suggestions, and their erroneous assumption of the good faith of the administration in its claim of interest in negotiations, made them vulnerable to a token gesture which would test nothing. This President Johnson shrewdly supplied, over the opposition of Secretaries Rusk and McNamara, who reportedly felt that the suspension "would only cast doubt on U.S. determination to maintain a free [sic] South Vietnam."

President Johnson showed his superior political acumen by the course taken. A five-day lull would hardly give the enemy time to respond; and response would be discouraged if we informed the North Vietnamese that the lull would quickly be ended if they failed to promptly halt their "aggression" in South Vietnam. If the North Vietnamese still insisted on responding, this too could be deftly turned aside, as was done in April. Meanwhile,

---

[21] Strafing attacks on North Vietnam were continued during this period.

[22] Tom Wicker, *New York Times,* May 19, 1965.

the doves who could not bring themselves to question the good intentions of the U.S. government would be neutralized.

On December 11, 1965, the North Vietnamese published the text of the note which they had received from Secretary Rusk on May 12th.[23] The reason for the failure of the State Department to make this document public is plainly evident. It is not only bullying in tone, but it expresses open disbelief that the bombing lull was likely to be useful. The note announced a "pause" in the bombings for "a limited trial period" during which North Vietnam had to make "significant reductions" in "armed actions" which it was alleged to control.[24] The note then went on to threaten heavier and more destructive air attacks if the North Vietnamese did not come forth with the proper response. It is important to realize that the U.S. note *did not call for a response in the form of a willingness to discuss or negotiate.* It demanded a halt in alleged aggression by North Vietnam. This was in no sense a peace feeler by the United States; it was an ultimatum to surrender. Yet it was presented to the American public as a test of Hanoi's interest in "discussions" and "negotiations."

Once again the North Vietnamese *did respond.* On the fifth day of the bombing lull, a North Vietnamese representative in Paris asked the French government to transmit a message to the United

---

[23] Shortly after May 12th, Washington passed the word that Canadian officials were involved in this diplomatic move—presumably an effort on the part of Washington to lend its move a measure of international approval. On May 23, however, the *Times* reported that "Paul Martin, [Canadian] Minister of External Affairs, has denied Washington reports that Canada served in any way as a messenger to Hanoi." ("U.S. Irks Canada by Vietnam Move," *New York Times*, May 23, 1965.) A similar and equally misleading attempt to implicate the Canadians in failure of a U.S. peace move occurred in June 1966, as we discuss in the next chapter.

[24] *New York Times*, Dec. 12, 1965. It is amusing to contrast Mr. Goldberg's defense of major U.S. air attacks on North Vietnam *over three weeks* after the Hanoi peace feeler of November 20, on the ground that such bombings are planned "weeks in advance," and presumably cannot be called off, with the American insistence in May that Hanoi demonstrate a significant reduction in armed actions in South Vietnam in *five days.* The contrast is understandable only if it is recognized that in neither instance was the United States interested in actual negotiations.

States, informing it of North Vietnam's readiness to discuss or negotiate on the basis of the "four points" put forward by Hanoi on April 8th (and which Max Frankel reported in August were regarded in Washington as in part "acceptable" and in part in need of "refinement"). American correspondent David Schoenbrun stated that he was informed by a "French government official in highest authority" that this North Vietnamese offer was for "unconditional negotiations on a Vietnamese cease fire." [25] More recently, columnist Joseph Kraft reported that the North Vietnamese reply made it clear that the prior withdrawal of U.S. troops was *not* called for, and that "the highest French officials" considered the May response "to be an undoubted opening for further exploration." [26]

In this instance the Hanoi response was handled by Washington in the following way: The North Vietnamese were of course rebuffed, but the fact of the response was not communicated to the American people (exactly as was the case with the U Thant efforts in the fall of 1964). [27] It was brought to public attention only in October and November of 1965, by Donald Keys, Sanford Gottlieb, and Schoenbrun. The Hanoi reply was then acknowledged by the State Department with the explanation that the reply had been received several days after the renewal of the bombings [28] and that it contained nothing beyond the four point proposal of April 8th. Besides, a State Department official informed Mr. Gottlieb, the Hanoi response was "not the message we were looking for." As we have pointed out, the State Department's note of May 12th makes it plain that the message desired

---

[25] *Philadelphia Inquirer,* Nov. 17, 1965.

[26] *Philadelphia Bulletin,* Jan. 5, 1966.

[27] At the end of the lull, State Department Press Officer Robert McCloskey stated flatly that there had been "no reaction" by Hanoi. (*New York Times,* May 19, 1965.)

[28] This appears to be another State Department misrepresentation. In his press conference of Jan. 21, 1966, Secretary Rusk contradicted the original State Department explanation when he stated that "In May [1965] there was a cessation of bombing which ended *after* a harsh rejection by the other side of any serious move toward peace." There are other indications that the North Vietnamese response was made the day before the United States resumed its bombings.

was not a willingness to negotiate but a cessation of "aggression."

But it is clear that Hanoi *did* reply, that the fact of reply was kept from the American public, and that no attempt was made to clarify the issues by any counter-proposals or suggestions. It thus seems that once again North Vietnam called the American bluff. But once again, also it was unable to prevent the Johnson administration from converting an obvious public relations effort, surely not intended to result in either "discussions" or "negotiations," into what the *New York Times* described editorially (May 20) as "another demonstration both to American opinion and to the world that Washington was prepared to be flexible and reasonable"!

President Johnson's press conference statement of July 28, 1965, along with his appointment of Mr. Justice Goldberg to the post of United Nations Ambassador (vacated by the death of Adlai Stevenson), constituted a high point in public relations efforts aimed at the camouflaging of a win policy. For the first time the President gave explicit verbal support to free elections in South Vietnam "or throughout all Vietnam under international supervision." He declared his readiness to discuss Hanoi's proposals, although he referred repeatedly to the conflict as one caused simply by "Communist aggression." No specific proposal was made on the matter of elections, and no suggestion of a truce was offered. Left unexplained was why the avowed readiness to discuss Hanoi's proposals had been so long delayed. Most fundamentally, there was no hint of any willingness to recognize the indigenous character of the NLF and to deal with it as an important political force in South Vietnam.

Nevertheless, the verbal concessions to free elections and unification were once again sufficient to disorganize much of the administration's political opposition, despite the vagueness of President Johnson's statement, its remarkable hypocrisy ("we will continue as best we can to help the good people of South

---

See the A.P. report of Nov. 17, 1965; *New York Times*, Nov. 18, 1965; and Jean Lacouture, *Vietnam Between Two Truces*, pp. 282-83. The authors of *The Politics of Escalation* are thus led to conclude: "From this it would seem that the North Vietnamese message, instead of arriving too late, may actually have been the cause for the resumption of bombing" (p. 66).

Vietnam enrich the condition of their life"), and the widening contradiction between words and deeds.

In the world of *deeds,* the statement of July 28th announced and was followed by a large buildup of U.S. arms and manpower in South Vietnam. And there was once again a marked intensification of air attacks on North Vietnam.[29] Since neither of these actions could have been expected to increase the enemy's willingness to negotiate (and they did not have that effect), it seems clear that negotiations were neither sought nor intended. One may safely conclude that the July 28th statement, and the Goldberg appointment, were mainly intended to make palatable (or perhaps to obscure) the fact that the United States was significantly escalating the war in mid-summer. More than this, by September 1965 the war was obviously becoming the fully "American war" against which President Kennedy had warned (but had been the first to begin to implement). Accordingly, there is no evidence whatever to suggest either a change in the U.S. objective of a non-Communist South Vietnam affiliated with us, or a willingness to soften total opposition to political concessions to the enemy.

Following the July 28th statement, there appears to have been some discussion in official circles of a possible mutual de-escalation that might permit an extended cease fire and negotiations. How seriously this line of thought was pursued in Washington is not known, but it may have prompted Secretary Rusk's suggestion that a withdrawal of the 325th Division by North Vietnam might initiate a de-escalation process. North Vietnam quickly denied that the 325th was in South Vietnam and the matter lapsed. But on August 20th, Max Frankel stated in the *New York Times* that "There were indications that the Vietcong

---

[29] In the six month period from Feb. 6 to Aug. 5, 1965, there were roughly 1,000 air attacks on North Vietnam; in the two months between Aug. 6 and Oct. 10, there were over 1,000 such attacks. That indicates an approximate tripling of the rate of bombings after the President's "peace" speech of July 28. (Jacques Decornoy, in *Le Monde,* Oct. 28-Nov. 3, 1965.) It has also been revealed that the planned step-up in military action after July 28 was so large that the anticipated casualties were greater than those actually incurred. (Jack Raymond, *New York Times,* Dec. 17, 1965.)

had not recently received any major new infusions of men and supplies from North Vietnam." And on September 21 and 22 the *Washington Star,* the *Washington Post,* and the *St. Louis Post Dispatch* all reported that the 325th Division had not been contacted by U.S. Intelligence for several weeks. The State Department denied that the Division had been withdrawn, but acknowledged that it had not engaged in military activity for some time. It would seem, then, that North Vietnam again responded to a U.S. appeal, this time with deeds. The U.S. counter-response was further military escalation. As we shall see below, this pattern of publicly calling for a military response by the enemy and then ignoring it when it occurs was even more obvious during the "peace offensive" of January 1966.

As American participation in the Vietnam war expanded in the summer and fall of 1965, a new vested interest in plans, contracts, supplies, and the like tended to give the war a more self-propelling character. "Jet airfields, docks, roads, bridges, military quarters and even a city are being built by thousands of men and women and hundreds of earth-moving machines. . . . Never before in any war, according to officers in charge here, has so much construction work been planned for one country in so short a time. By late next summer most of the projects now started or still in the planning stage are expected to be largely finished."[30] The U.S. buildup spread rapidly into Thailand as well.[31] At Sattahip the United States had under construction a naval base large enough to accommodate the entire Seventh Fleet. This snowballing military-industrial program would be hard to defuse even with a real interest in a peaceful settlement in Washington.

Although President Johnson has reiterated that "we seek neither territory nor bases" (let alone a "wider war"), there have been many, and in the aggregate persuasive, reports suggesting

---

[30] Hanson Baldwin, writing from Saigon, *New York Times,* Nov. 28, 1965.

[31] See Seymour Topping, *New York Times,* Dec. 12, 1965, and Feb. 20, 1966; Hanson Baldwin, *New York Times,* Feb. 4, 1966; and Alex Campbell, "Thailand," *New Republic,* March 26, 1966.

a long range purpose in the American military buildup in Vietnam. James Reston pointed out on August 27, 1965:

"The United States bases and supply areas are being constructed on a scale far larger than is necessary to care for the present level of American forces—therefore it is assumed that the buildup will continue well beyond what has been announced so far.

"In fact, the United States base at Camranh, which has one of the best natural ports in Asia, is being developed into another Okinawa, not merely for the purposes of war, but as a major power complex from which American officials hope a wider alliance of Asian nations, with the help of the United States, will eventually be able to contain the expansion of China."

In January 1966, Pierre Darcourt stated that by 1972 Camranh will be "the most spacious [air-naval base] in the Pacific"; [32] and Drew Pearson reported that this base was being built for "a 20 to 30 year occupation" of South Vietnam. [33] Francois Sully, *Newsweek's* veteran reporter on Southeast Asia, described U.S. construction activities in Vietnam as part of a permanent military buildup aimed at encircling China. In this respect "By far the biggest U.S. construction effort . . . is in South Vietnam itself . . . Currently the Pentagon insists that these bases will be abandoned when the fighting in Vietnam ends, but it is an interesting fact that, legally, the U.S. is obligated to return them to the Saigon government 'when no longer needed.' " [34]

The rapid buildup and initial combat successes of American troops (operating with unlimited air support and the most modern weaponry) also served to bring into the open the feeling that, militarily, the United States definitely can "win" in South Vietnam. After the significant expansion of U.S. military power in Vietnam and the introduction of widespread use of B-52 satu-

---

[32] *L'Express*, Jan. 2, 1966.

[33] *New York Post*, Dec. 24, 1965.

[34] *Newsweek*, Jan. 31, 1966. In June 1966 there were reports in Saigon that the Ky government had given the United States a 99 year lease on the giant Camranh base (Robert Guillain, *Le Monde*, May 26-June 1, 1966).
Detailed 1966 accounts of the long-term planning behind the

ration bombing of "suspected Vietcong strongholds" in the summer of 1965, a new chorus of "the tide has turned" exultations began to resound.

Even among more professional and comparatively sober men the same story began to be heard. In late October, General Maxwell Taylor stated that success in South Vietnam could be attained by the destruction and dissolution of the enemy, with neither formal surrender nor any negotiations ever needed; the dying and decimated Vietcong would presumably "just peter out." [35] Lieut. General B. E. Spivey, a top military planner for the Joint Chiefs of Staff, indicated in a speech in Chicago in mid-November that the real aim of the United States is to pour in so much fire power that "the Communists will be worn out"; they will be so beaten down that they will be "run downhill toward military ineffectiveness and defeat." [36] More importantly, this position was taken by Secretary of State Rusk, who on October 16 went so far as to say (off the record) that our policy in South Vietnam was no longer one of negotiations but military victory. This led Senator Mansfield to deliver a Senate speech on October 19, attacking "certain anonymous government officials" who were suggesting that the United States was now pursuing a total "win" policy. (Senator Mansfield was mistaken; an implicit policy was simply being made more explicit).

During the fall of 1965 a steady stream of reports from Washington indicated that with the "dampening of the peace bloc" and the "braked" pressures for a peaceful settlement, negotiations had been definitely pushed into the background. "The word is being passed by highly credible sources," Robert Roth reported, " that we don't want negotiations now, that we would much prefer to wait until later when our position is likely to be

---

"hard" military buildup of the United States in Vietnam may be found in *Newsweek*, January 31; *Business Week*, March 5; Hanson Baldwin, "U.S. Construction to Hit Peak in Summer," *New York Times*, April 10; "U.S. in Vietnam Builds Up, and Up, and Up," *New York Times*, June 19; and E. K. Faltermayer, "The Surprising Aspects of South Vietnam's Economy," *Fortune*, March.

[35] *New York Times*, Oct. 28, 1965.

[36] *Philadelphia Bulletin*, Nov. 16, 1965.

even stronger and the settlement we can get will be more to
our liking than might now be possible." [37] Nonetheless, throughout the fall of 1965 the public position of the Johnson administration was that *we* were always ready to talk, but the other
side remained stubborn.

---

[37] *Philadelphia Bulletin*, Sept. 26, 1965.

V

THE DIPLOMACY OF A "WIN POLICY" (II)

Further confirmation of our analysis of public relations diplomacy was furnished by Washington's handling of the Hanoi peace feeler communicated to President Johnson by Amintore Fanfani, Italian Foreign Minister and United Nations General Assembly President, on November 20, 1965. Two Italian citizens known to Fanfani visited North Vietnam in early November, 1965, and spoke at length with Ho Chi Minh and other high officials. They were informed that the government of North Vietnam was strongly desirous of peace, and they were given a detailed statement of Hanoi's conditions for the initiation of peace negotiations. These Italians communicated this information to Fanfani, who in turn transmitted it to President Johnson in the Fanfani note.

The Fanfani note indicated that Ho Chi Minh was quite as ready as President Johnson to "go anywhere"; that prior withdrawal of American troops was *not* a precondition for peace talks; and that a general cessation of belligerent actions and some indication of American acceptance of the Geneva Agreements were the only requirements for discussions.

This promising feeler was clearly distasteful to Washington, and, following the receipt of the note, the administration pursued a course of action that can be interpreted only as deliberate, *de facto* rejection. That the note was unwelcome is evident from the fact that Secretary Rusk's response to Fanfani, unaccountably delayed for over two weeks, was distinctly negative in tone. Rusk was "far from persuaded" of a "real willingness for unconditional negotiations," and so forth. This lack of interest is confirmed by the fact that when Richard Dudman, a Washington correspondent of the *St. Louis Post-Dispatch,* inquired about the matter, an "authoritative source" in the State Department gave the "wholly negative response, 'we are not taking this seriously.' "[1]

---

[1] Quoted by Arthur Krock, *New York Times,* Dec. 21, 1965.

Furthermore, this negativism and evasion repeated a familiar pattern. According to Hella Pick:

". . . many UN diplomatists have been recalling that the Foreign Minister of Hungary, Mr. Janos Peter, who visited the UN General Assembly in October, had essentially the same message which the Italians brought—namely, that Hanoi no longer made it a precondition to negotiations that U.S. troops must be evacuated.

"What was demanded, and still is, is a cessation of the bombing and a halt to fresh U.S. troop landings. Mr. Peter had just returned from a trip to Southeast Asia, and had met Vietnamese leaders. Unimpeachable UN sources satisfied themselves at the time that Mr. Peter was in fact acting as an emissary from Hanoi and was transmitting the same kind of message which the two Italians have now brought back from Hanoi.

"Mr. Peter saw Mr. Rusk; nevertheless the Secretary of State insisted at the time that Mr. Peter appeared only to be expressing his personal views, and Mr. Goldberg, the U.S. Ambassador to the UN, on Friday reiterated that the Hungarian Foreign Minister had not brought an authorized message. UN diplomatists are not prepared to accept this at its face value. They see a certain pattern in U.S. responses—or lack of responses." [2]

Washington's lack of interest in negotiations is also apparent in the manner in which the confidential Fanfani-Rusk communications were made public, despite the certainty of a damaging effect on diplomacy. The *St. Louis Post-Dispatch* story relating to Fanfani's efforts was published only after Dudman had been informed by the State Department that the matter was not being taken seriously. "No official request to withhold the publication was made to the newspaper until it had already appeared . . .," although the State Department was forewarned of publication.[3] The administration's pretense that release of the docu-

---

[2] "Doubts Over U.S. Good Faith on Vietnam," *Manchester Guardian Weekly*, Dec. 23, 1965.

[3] Arthur Krock, *loc. cit.* Hella Pick also personally established that the *St. Louis Post-Dispatch* had not been requested to suppress the story (*loc. cit.*). This casts considerable doubt on the validity of the statement made by Ambassador Goldberg in the United Na-

ments was forced upon it by factors outside its control thus
appears to be still another fabrication.[4]

Subsequent events were even more revealing. After Washington's receipt of the Fanfani note on November 20, Hanoi was,
of course, awaiting some kind of reply. It was delivered in two
stages. First, U.S. bombings were intensified;[5] then they were
significantly extended into the Hanoi-Haiphong industrial complex for the first time (the vital Uong Bi electric power station
at Haiphong). Arthur Krock called these bombings a "unique
way of getting 'clarification' of an enemy's possible shift to peaceful intent . . ."[6]

The timing of these bombings is especially significant, for they
took place just when Secretary Rusk was at last sending Hanoi
an answer to the Fanfani note. On December 13th Fanfani notified Rusk that Hanoi had received Rusk's transmitted reply.
Little more than a day later the United States bombed the
Uong Bi power station. What is more, these air attacks were
carried out *after* Washington had received explicit warnings that
such attacks would doom any chances for negotiations. Hella
Pick states that it was known at the United Nations "that President Johnson was personally informed that the bombing of Hanoi
or Haiphong would automatically close the door to this approach."[7] Donald Grant, U.N. correspondent for the *St. Louis
Post-Dispatch*, points out that in a conversation with one of the

---

tions that the *Post-Dispatch* had been asked to consider whether
publication was in the best interests of the United States.

[4] Max Frankel considers it "ironic" that many who criticized the
State Department for its past suppressions criticized it for having
released the Fanfani documents now. (*New York Times*, Dec. 26,
1965.) It does not seem to have occurred to Frankel that there is a
difference between the suppression of documents of previously rejected diplomatic exchanges, and the withholding of documents relating to currently active and sensitive negotiations. The difference
is basic.

[5] "United States pilots subjected North Vietnam yesterday and
early today to the most intensive bombardment of the war." (R.
W. Apple, "U.S. Presses Raids on North Vietnam," *New York Times*,
Dec. 10, 1965.)

[6] *Loc. cit.*   [7] *Loc. cit.*

Italian citizens (La Pira) "Ho had stated explicitly that any air strike in the Haiphong-Hanoi area would end the possibility of peace talks. Within hours after Rusk's note reached Hanoi the United States bombed the Haiphong power station." [8] Furthermore, it is now known that on December 8th Ambassador Goldberg had been personally warned "that Ho would not enter peace negotiations with the U.S. if the Hanoi-Haiphong area were bombed" [9]—a warning Goldberg undoubtedly communicated to Washington.

Ambassador Goldberg's rebuttal to all these observations, that "our bombing program is laid on weeks in advance," would be a crushing indictment of the competence of the Johnson administration if it were really interested in achieving a negotiated settlement. But Goldberg's statement flies in the face of Mr. Bundy's reference to the "insistent, direct surveillance which the President maintains over major military decisions, and *specifically over decisions which affect military action against North Vietnam*." [10]

It is difficult to avoid the conclusion that the bombing of the Haiphong power plant, the intensified regular bombings, the rapid American buildup in Thailand, and the talk of possible U.S. ground operations into Laos and Cambodia *all added up to a very deliberate signal to North Vietnam:* we are not interested in *real* negotiations; communicate with us only when you are prepared to let Generals Ky and Westmoreland pacify South Vietnam without "foreign" interference.

North Vietnam's disavowal of the Fanfani note on December 18 brought one more diplomatic effort to an unsuccessful conclusion. With the American buildup in South Vietnam and Thailand proceeding rapidly in December, it was evident that further U.S. escalation of the war was imminent.

---

[8] "Vietnam: The View from the United Nations," *Progressive*, April 1966.

[9] *St. Louis Post-Dispatch*, Dec. 29, 1965.

[10] Transcript of CBS-TV program of Aug. 23, 1965.

At that point, however, domestic and international confidence in Washington's avowed claims of interest in a negotiated settlement was again at a low ebb.[11] The Fanfani note episode had come hard on the heels of the administration's refusal to pursue the Janos Peter diplomatic feeler in October; and in November the credibility of the U.S. government was further undermined by the Sevareid-Stevenson revelations of administration rejection of two different negotiation efforts in the fall of 1964, and by the disclosure of the suppressed fact that Hanoi had indeed responded to the bombing lull of mid-May.

We have seen how domestic and external pressures, credibility crises, and the need to prepare the ground for greater escalation produced the earlier peace moves of the United States. Given the magnitude of the December 1965 credibility crisis, acceptance of the next phase of the Johnson policy required another public relations effort, greater than that of July 28 (which had greased the skids for the summer escalation).

To all indications, the administration adopted and shaped the new peace offensive in hastily improvised stages, commencing with a grudging acceptance of the NLF-proposed Christmas-New Year cease fire arrangements. Having been thus dragooned into the cease fire, and under considerable pressure to extend the bombing pause and to press for a negotiated settlement, Washington apparently decided to turn these sentiments to its own advantage by embarking on a major "peace offensive." This interlude may be dated from the cease fire of December 24, 1965 to the renewal of bombing raids on North Vietnam on February 1, 1966. Its basic ingredients were (1) a well publicized set of missions to several countries—whose primary function was to win support for U.S. policy by convincing the world of the sincerity of the American quest for peace; (2) a fourteen point

---

[11] According to Carl Rowan, a commentator sympathetic with administration actions in Vietnam, "My recent travels in the Midwest indicate that a public crisis in confidence is growing. That is, more and more Americans believe that the President is giving only lip service to peace." (*Philadelphia Bulletin*, Dec. 10, 1965.) Just prior to the peace offensive, Ambassador Goldberg admitted: "We have a great problem here maintaining credibility with our own people." (*New York Times*, Dec. 20, 1965.) See also, Max Frankel, "A Crisis of Confidence Confronts the U.S.," *New York Times*, Dec. 26, 1965.

statement summarizing the U.S. negotiating position on Vietnam; (3) a note transmitted to North Vietnam on December 29, the contents of which have not yet been made public; and (4) a "pause" in the bombing of North Vietnam.

Judging by all the relevant facts, this new "peace offensive" was no more intended to produce negotiations, or a cease fire, than the bombing lull of mid-May or the other U.S. peace moves previously discussed. The primary purpose of the new peace offensive appears to have been re-establishment of Washington's credibility in order to sustain the next stage of military escalation. This escalation could have been prevented only by an acknowledgment by Hanoi and the NLF of a willingness to surrender all claim to power in South Vietnam.

The essentially public relations character of the peace offensive is shown by the following nine points, which are elaborated upon in the succeeding paragraphs.

(1) The sabotaging by the Johnson administration of the Hanoi peace feelers of October and November; (2) the frank admission by the administration of the need for re-establishment of credibility, and the flamboyantly "public" character of the peace drive; (3) the absence of any hint of concession on NLF recognition and participation in government, and the failure to produce any constructive proposal for a cease fire, elections, or basis of settlement; (4) the reiterated commitments to the Ky government, and the uncontradicted reports of assurances given that government to the effect that negotiations would not be permitted to threaten its interests; (5) the large buildup of U.S. military forces during the peace offensive, and the numerous indications that the buildup would continue, presaging a long-term U.S. occupation of South Vietnam; (6) the deliberate U.S. escalation of the fighting in South Vietnam during the peace offensive, despite an acknowledged de-escalation by North Vietnam and the NLF; (7) the resumption of the bombing of North Vietnam, on grounds that appear to be remarkably thin if one assumed a genuine interest in a negotiated settlement; (8) the cynical resort to the United Nations *after* the resumption of the bombing of North Vietnam and *after* the United States administration had gone to great lengths to show the inappro-

priateness of a U.N. approach; (9) the Honolulu Conference
and the rapid shift to an open policy of victory.

(1) We have already discussed Washington's persistent negativism, and its sabotaging of the Peter peace feeler of October
and the Fanfani effort of late November. We have seen no
plausible explanation for the failure of the administration to ex-
plore these possible routes to negotiations, energetically and
privately, besides the one mentioned earlier—namely, that it
has been pursuing a win policy and has never been interested in
negotiations in any meaningful sense of the word.

(2) The fanfare that marked the peace offensive, described
by *Le Monde* as an "improvised publicity operation," reflected
its real character. In this instance the views of *Le Monde* were
in accord with those of Joseph Alsop, who bluntly stated that
"If President Johnson had really wanted negotiations . . . he
would have omitted the fanfare and tackled the problem in a
quietly professional manner." [12]

The missions of Harriman, Goldberg, Bundy, and Mennen Wil-
liams made imposing headlines, but their value as diplomatic
efforts to achieve a settlement in Vietnam appears to have been
quite intentionally nil. As early as January 2, 1966, Max Frankel
stated in the *New York Times* that "no new diplomatic offers are
being presented in these missions, [Washington] officials report."
Besides, Frankel added, the missions were "a virtually public
campaign of propaganda and psychological warfare to win support for the U.S. position and respect for its intentions."

The public relations essence of the peace offensive is also illustrated by the frankness of administration spokesmen in de-
scribing its role as one of re-establishing credibility. American
officials were understandably upset when "an ostensibly friendly
diplomat" referred to the ambassadorial missions as a "traveling
circus." [13] A similar view of these missions (and the later Asian
tour of Vice-President Humphrey) was expressed by the editors
of the *Wall Street Journal* (February 15), who described the
"diplomatic country-hopping" as an "unedifying spectacle."

President Johnson's February 1st remarks on renewing the

[12] *New York Herald Tribune*, Jan. 6, 1966.

[13] *New York Times*, Jan. 5, 1966.

bombing of North Vietnam offered additional evidence of the public relations role of the peace offensive: "We have given a full and decent respect to the opinions of those who thought that such a pause might give new hope for peace. . . . We have paused for twice the time suggested by some of those who urged it." This is not the language of a man "relentlessly" pursuing peace; it reveals a President impatient to get on with the business of winning the war, and righteously trying to impress the world with his concessions to public opinion.[14]

It should also be pointed out that a *public* campaign such as that the Johnson administration carried out during the peace offensive is in sharp conflict with a view common in diplomatic circles—that it would be difficult for Hanoi to respond to any open, public gesture by the United States, for fear of aggravating tensions between itself and Peking. This view was periodically acknowledged by Washington itself,[15] which nonetheless maintained the fiction that quiet diplomacy was compatible with (and was being pursued in the midst of) the publicity drive. In reality, however, resort by Washington to a "public campaign of propaganda and psychological warfare" was the counterpart of its earlier rejection of the Peter and Fanfani efforts to initiate a quiet diplomatic exchange. That widespread publicity would be destructive of negotiations by reducing the possibility of North Vietnamese cooperation was irrelevant to the administration. *The response Washington was looking for during the peace offensive was not from North Vietnam or the* NLF; it was concerned with obtaining support and respect for the position and intentions of the United States at home and in the world at large.

(3) The note the American Embassy in Rangoon, Burma, delivered to the North Vietnamese Embassy in Rangoon on December 29 has not been made public, but there is strong evidence that it included no new offers, concessions, or constructive pro-

---

[14] "The President, according to informed sources, never was too keen on the pause, to begin with. However, he saw it as an opportunity to persuade foreign capitals and public opinion at home that he was serious about the search for a peaceful solution to the conflict in Vietnam." (John Pomfret, *New York Times*, Feb. 1, 1966.)

[15] "U.S. is Searching for Hanoi Reply," *New York Times*, Dec. 28, 1965.

posals that would make a conference seem useful to Hanoi. We have noted Max Frankel's statement that the ambassadors to the various capitals made "no new diplomatic offers." Washington's "fourteen points", published in the early days of the peace offensive to present in a more formal manner the negotiating position of the United States,[16] simply gathered together statements made by the administration at one time or another in the past; they added nothing new. Some of the fourteen points overlap terms announced by Hanoi and the NLF, but disagreements remained particularly over the role of the NLF and the organization of any elections. Hanoi and the NLF could not possibly agree to an election to be held under the auspices of General Ky.[17] An election, even under international supervision, would have to be held under the local authority of an interim coalition government that would include the NLF. This would require negotiating with the NLF and admitting it to a provisional government. During the peace offensive the United States made no concessions on these critical matters. In fact, Secretary Rusk continued to maintain his rigid position that peace can be brought about *only* if Hanoi is "going to hold its hand and refrain from trying to impose a political solution on South Vietnam by force." This was the "central issue" for Rusk, who remains unyieldingly against negotiations with the NLF. There is no evidence that Johnson disagrees with his chief foreign policy officer on this point.

In commenting on the peace offensive, Walter Lippman observed that the "whole spectacular business" would be regarded as "the device of a showman" if the administration failed to make its peace terms consistent with the realities of Southeast Asia. One of these realities, which Lippmann sees as the "central issue," is a willingness "to negotiate a truce with the main adversary

---

[16] The fourteen points may be found in the *New York Times*, Jan. 2, 1966.

[17] General Ky has made it known on several occasions that his idea of free elections is one in which the NLF would be prohibited from taking part; see Charles Mohr, "Ky Moves Up Date for Constitution," *New York Times*, March 26, 1966, and Ch. II (notes 15 and 16).

in the field, the Vietcong." [18] Similarly, on January 20th, in an unusual statement apparently born of desperation, Secretary General U Thant suggested that "concrete proposals" by the United States on a representative coalition government, presumably including the NLF, might hasten negotiations. All of these suggestions were ignored, *because the realities of Southeast Asia are themselves unacceptable to the Johnson administration.* Its objective, an "independent" South Vietnam, requires a new reality that it seeks to create by sheer force of arms—a reality that will necessitate the virtual extermination of the NLF and the large portion of the rural population which supports it.

(4) The Saigon cliques have been unalterably opposed to any negotiations, for an obvious reason: their domestic support is so meager that their survival is not only contingent upon a massive U.S. presence, it is also threatened by the very rumors of a peaceful settlement.[19] During the peace offensive the United States reassured the Saigon government of the strength of our commitment to it. The most impressive evidence on this point was provided in the report of Gavin Young in the London *Observer* of January 16, 1966.[20] Young interviewed South Vietnamese Foreign Minister Tran Van Do the day before the arrival of Secretary Rusk in Saigon. He was told that the United States had given Saigon "a firm undertaking" not to negotiate so long as NLF and North Vietnamese troops remain in South Vietnam, and "firm

---

[18] *Philadelphia Inquirer*, Jan. 4, 1966.

[19] On several occasions General Ky and his colleagues have stated their absolute opposition to any discussions with the NLF. See Ky's statement that he "would never sit down at a negotiating table with the Communist aggressors" (*New York Times*, Nov. 12, 1965); Charles Mohr's *New York Times* report of Feb. 9, 1966, "South Vietnamese Chiefs Bar Talks with Vietcong"; the May 7, 1966 remarks of General Ky, in which he said he "would stand and fight" against any freely elected *neutralist* forces that might negotiate with the NLF; and Ky's answer to American journalists who asked him about the possibility of negotiations with the Communists: "If the Vietcong is prepared to surrender, negotiation is no longer necessary" (*Philadelphia Bulletin*, July 5, 1966).

[20] For other reports of U.S. assurances to Saigon, see Richard Eder, *New York Times*, Dec. 28 and Dec. 29, 1965.

assurances" never to recognize the NLF in any case. Rusk's expressions of full support for the Saigon government on January 16th[21] led Hanoi to point out immediately that Washington's commitments to the Saigon cliques amount to establishing conditions on the "unconditional discussions," and preclude any discussions whatsoever.[22]

President **Johnson and Ambassador Goldberg** have suggested that the apparent intransigence of the Saigon military juntas (including the Ky government) is for South Vietnamese domestic consumption only, and is irrelevant to the success or failure of our own efforts for negotiations. But since a Saigon government would have to be a party to any negotiations, its position can hardly be regarded as irrelevant by North Vietnam, by the NLF, or by objective observers. In evaluating the sincerity of Mr. Johnson's quest for peace it is significant that the Saigon government has maintained a position of total opposition to a negotiated settlement and has, moreover, received unswerving support from the government of the United States.[23]

(5) Although the peace offensive was terminated and the bombings of North Vietnam resumed on the ground that the enemy had used the pause to build up his armed forces, Jack Raymond reported in the *New York Times* that Washington officials estimated "that the rate of infiltration during the lull had not exceeded the peak of 4500 men a month that it had reached about the time the bombings were suspended."[24] Confirming that there had been no speedup in the infiltration, Daniel Hoffman

---

[21] Mr. Joseph Alsop described the effects of Rusk's visit and statements as "calming and reassuring" for the Saigon generals. (*Philadelphia Bulletin*, Jan. 26, 1966.)

[22] "Hanoi Bars Talks Till U.S. Ends Aid," *New York Times*, Jan. 17, 1966.

[23] It is also revealing that during his February visit to Southeast Asia, "Mr. Humphrey assured [top Thai officials] . . . that there had been no attempt at Honolulu to press South Vietnam into quick peace talks. Neither was there any attempt to force it to accept the Vietcong as a party at the bargaining table, he said." (Seth King, *New York Times*, Feb. 14, 1966.)

[24] *New York Times*, Feb. 1, 1966. See also the U.P.I. report of C. W. Cordry, Jan. 31, 1966.

added that U.S. officials also doubted that there had been any substantial increase in anti-aircraft or missile emplacements in North Vietnam during the pause.[25]

On the other hand, the United States appears to have increased its own military forces by at least 14,000 men during the last fourteen days of the pause alone.[26] On January 18, 7,000 U.S. combat troops were reported landing in South Vietnam, bringing the total to 190,000; and Associated Press reported on January 29 that a level of "over 197,000" had been reached. These man-power increases were paralleled by a huge inflow of weapons and materiel to U.S. and South Vietnamese forces. On balance, "our own official estimates indicate that the U.S. and South Vietnam brought in substantially more supplies during the pause than did the enemy." [27] Once again the deeds of the Johnson administration contradicted its peaceable words and revealed the public relations function of the "peace offensive."

(6) That function is revealed with even greater clarity by U.S. military activities in South Vietnam. The opening of the peace offensive was followed by a series of major offensives, *successively designated* as the largest American operations of the war. The U.S.-Australian Ho Bo Forest sweep of January 8-9, "the largest offensive operation of the Vietnam war," a "record sweep," was followed by the large-scale Marine amphibious landings in Quang Ngai province (the largest Marine landings since the Korean war), and the even bigger "Operation Masher" in the jungles 290 miles northeast of Saigon.[28] In addition, U.S. bomb-

---

[25] *Philadelphia Inquirer*, Feb. 1, 1966; confirmed by John Norris, *Washington Post*, Feb. 1, 1966.

[26] It will be noted that in these two weeks the United States added more troops than the North Vietnamese are alleged to infiltrate into South Vietnam in three months, and only slightly fewer than the total number of North Vietnamese regulars claimed to be in South Vietnam in December 1965.

[27] James Reston, *New York Times*, Feb. 1, 1966. Reston's colleague Arthur Krock commented that "Perhaps . . . 37 days was as long as our own military position in Vietnam could be improved faster than Hanoi's." (*Ibid.*)

[28] *Philadelphia Inquirer*, Jan. 9, 1966; *New York Times*, Jan. 10 and Jan. 30, 1966. The Ho Bo sweep was carried out along with a

ings of Laos were intensified during the peace offensive period.[29]

In his State of the Union Message of January 12, President Johnson stated that "we'll respond if others reduce their use of force. . . ." But precisely while the United States was mounting this succession of "largest" military operations in South Vietnam, the North Vietnamese and NLF appear to have been scaling down their own use of force. The early January rumors to this effect in Saigon were substantiated by President Johnson in his press conference of January 13. In response to a question whether "the other side in Vietnam is . . . reducing the intensity of the war at all," the President answered: "The number of incidents have dropped off some. I don't say that there is any connection with that and our peace moves, but that is a fact."

On January 17th, a report from Saigon indicated that there had been no recent contact with North Vietnamese units, and a Defense Department spokesman confirmed that the North Vietnamese had been "quiescent." In late January there were also said to be "indications that some units of the North Vietnamese army had pulled back across the South Vietnamese border into Laos and Cambodia."[30] And on January 27th Anthony Day stated in the *Philadelphia Bulletin* that "There have been reports from Saigon that the Vietcong has not engaged in any large battles since the Oriental New Year ended last Sunday (Jan. 23)." On the following day U.P.I. claimed that U.S. and South Vietnamese military intelligence had intercepted a message ordering North Vietnamese and NLF main forces units to effect a general scale-down in fighting. This was confirmed by "highly placed

---

tight withholding of information from the South Vietnamese forces until after operations were under way—illuminating testimony to the status of the supposedly independent government of South Vietnam and to the MacNamara-Taylor contention that our South Vietnamese allies are shouldering the major part of the fight "to protect themselves from Communist aggression."

[29] *New York Times*, Jan. 9 and Jan. 23, 1966.

[30] *New York Herald Tribune*, Jan. 29, 1966.

[31] *Ibid.*; and *Philadelphia Daily News*, Jan. 28, 1966.

On Jan. 31 Secretary Rusk was asked "to interpret the fact that there's been no large-scale direct contact with North Vietnamese troops since the latter part of November."

military sources" in Saigon which added that the Communists
had been told explicitly to avoid large battles with Americans.[31]

How did the United States respond to this apparent further de-
escalation? On January 28th U.P.I. reported the "heaviest fighting of the year" to be in progress, adding: "American military
spokesmen in Saigon said *the Americans picked the fight*. The
report came soon after disclosure of indications that the commanders of some North Vietnamese and regular Vietcong units
had been ordered to scale down their activities and avoid large
scale battles with American and allied forces in South Vietnam." [32]

Thus once again the record suggests that the enemy responded
to an American gesture with deeds—a significant de-escalation
of military operations in South Vietnam. And despite President
Johnson's promise to "respond if others reduce their use of force,"
American actions were on the contrary escalated to a substantial
degree. This seems to us solid proof of the public relations function of the peace offensive and of the intent of the Johnson administration to fight for total military victory.

(7) The principal reason given for renewal of the bombings
of North Vietnam was the desire to maintain our military securi-

---

Rusk's reply: "Well, there's some ambiguity about that. There
seems to have been some contact sometimes in December and there
are indications at the present time that there is very active contact
with North Vietnamese forces there." (*New York Times*, Feb. 1,
1966.)

The evasiveness of Rusk's reply is underscored by the reports
cited above; the last part of his statement is flatly contradicted by a
dispatch from Saigon a day later, that there had been another de-
cline in enemy activity noted by U.S. military authorities. (*Philadelphia Bulletin*, Feb. 2, 1966.)

[32] *Philadelphia Bulletin*, Jan. 28, 1966. See also the report in the
New York Times, Jan. 28, 1966, on how six U.S. battalions were sent
through Binhdinh province to "look for a battle."

In a letter to Frank Corner, U.N. Security Council President,
Ambassador Arthur Goldberg explained the extension of U.S.
bombings to Hanoi and Haiphong in June 1966 by stating that the
North Vietnamese response to "repeated and increased efforts" by
the United States to open peace negotiations had regularly been
"an accelerated tempo" of military activity. (*New York Times*,
July 1, 1966.) Goldberg's statement is contradicted by a wide
variety of official Washington sources—as well as by what is presented in our own text above.

ty and to save American lives. But since intensified warfare was
certain to result in increases in U.S. casualties,[33] the abandonment
of the peace drive made sense as a life saving device only if the
administration had no intention of negotiating on conditions the
enemy could accept. As Max Frankel has pointed out, "there
is reason to believe that the President and his senior aides, in
their own conception of negotiations, are not prepared to yield
more than an honorable Communist withdrawal from the battlefield."[34] In other words, since North Vietnam and the NLF do
not appear ready to surrender in anticipation of more destructive American escalation, "negotiations" are out of the question.

(8) Simultaneous with its renewing the bombing of North
Vietnam, the Johnson administration unexpectedly announced
it was putting the Vietnam question before the United Nations.
This was a tactical error. "If a Security Council debate was not
indicated during the bombing pause," as Donald Grant, U.N.
correspondent of the *St. Louis Post-Dispatch* wrote, "many diplomats found President Johnson's action positively grotesque in
linking an order to resume the bombings with his direction to
Goldberg to place the Vietnam issue before the Council."[35] In
fact, the very crudity of this maneuver and the obviousness of
its public relations purpose of softening the blow of renewed
bombings tended to reinforce doubts about earlier administration "peace" moves.

Previously Washington had gone to great lengths to explain
why the United Nations was not a useful device for bringing peace to Vietnam. In addition, since neither North Vietnam,

---

[33] For example, in the nine-month period from July 1965 to March
1966, the period of major escalation of air attacks against North
Vietnam and of "hunter-killer" ground operations in South Vietnam, over 2,000 American servicemen were reported killed in action.
This represents over three-fourths of the total number of U.S. combat deaths in South Vietnam since January 1961. And as escalation
in 1966 surpasses that of 1965, so American combat deaths rise accordingly. In the first 99 days of 1966 more U.S. servicemen were
killed in action than in all of 1965 (1,361 against 1,342). (*New
York Times*, April 16, 1966.)

[34] *New York Times*, Feb. 12, 1966. See also Frankel's remarks six
days later, quoted in Ch. II (note 28).

[35] *Op. cit.*

the NLF, nor China belongs to the United Nations, and since China itself had just been barred from U.N. membership once again by the strenuous efforts of the United States, the United Nations has hardly looked like a promising avenue of approach.

The United States was barely able to get the Vietnam issue onto the agenda of the Security Council when Ambassador Goldberg engineered an indefinite postponement of meetings on the subject. His reported hope that backdoor consultations at the United Nations might turn up something was demolished by the proceedings at the Honolulu Conference.

(9) Having exhausted its patience with the trying business of demonstrating its desire for peace, the administration returned to its win policy with vigor. That was the meaning of the Honolulu Conference of February 7 and 8, 1966.

By all accounts the President was in a militant mood, one certainly reflected in his opening speech on February 7. Rarely before had he so thoroughly embraced the "Munich" analogy of the "struggle against Communist aggression"; and his sharp attack on both foreign and domestic critics of his Vietnam policy went well beyond the bounds of mere annoyance at the idea of dissent.

The chief feature of the Conference was the further commitment made to General Ky and his military government, thereby strengthening an alliance widely recognized as incompatible with a negotiated settlement in Vietnam. This feature was underlined by the obvious manner in which Ky's opposition to negotiations with the NLF kept coming to the fore. Charles Mohr referred to "the attempt of the South Vietnamese to make clear to President Johnson their almost desperate desire not to be pushed into peace negotiations, or even into peace, until they are more able to compete politically with the Vietnamese Communists." [36] Also notable was that while the separate U.S. conference statement pledges support for "measures of social revolution, including land reform," the South Vietnamese statement makes no mention of land reform. In other words, the military clique supported by the United States scarcely pretends that

---

[36] "Honolulu Aftermath," *New York Times*, Feb. 11, 1966.

it wants to "compete politically" with the NLF; it prefers to rely on the force of U.S. arms.

These developments stood out above the closing "Declaration of Honolulu," a grab-bag of promises to "prevent aggression," to "establish and maintain a stable, viable economy and build a better material life for our people," and "to bring about a true social revolution."

The Honolulu Conference terminated the "relentless" search for peace promised during the great peace offensive and emphasized once more that President Johnson's *most* "sincere" intention in Vietnam is to win a military victory of sufficient dimension to permit General Ky (or some acceptable, militant anti-Communist substitute) to retain power. The *New York Times* offered this assessment of the conference: "The outlook is for war and more war, with no end anywhere in sight." [37]

Given the evidence available at present, the same cycle appears to have repeated itself in May and June of 1966. In late April, Pauline Frederick, National Broadcasting Company U.N. correspondent, reported a new Hanoi probing of American diplomatic intentions. Soviet sources at the United Nations stated that North Vietnam would enter into "unconditional" peace talks if all bombing of North Vietnam were ended. The questions of U.S. troop withdrawal and NLF representation could be taken up later; "they could be worked out." Miss Frederick was told by State Department officials that they would examine the report with "interest." [38]

At the end of May came the *Newsweek* report that North Vietnam had "moved to start peace talks, using Rumanian intermediaries," and that "U.S. officials have no independent cor-

---

[37] Feb. 13, 1966. The spirit of Honolulu was still evident in the President's Feb. 16 speech in Atlantic City. "His prepared address, notable for its uncompromising toughness in scoring the Vietcong, omitted the general hope for a negotiated settlement that had been featured in his recent talks." (Homer Bigart, *New York Times*, Feb. 17, 1966.)

[38] *New York Times*, April 23, 1966.

roboration of the story but regard it as probable."[39] White House Press Secretary Bill Moyers responded that he had "nothing on that." Then C.B.S. *World News* reported on June 7th that there had been a definite reduction in the number of enemy incidents in South Vietnam—the fewest in any month since the war began. U.S. officials expressed "surprise" at this development, especially since the Communists had been expected to launch a major "monsoon offensive" at this time.

Although none of these developments changed Washington's insistence that North Vietnam still refused to negotiate, others interested in a peaceful settlement took a different view. A new round of diplomatic efforts was begun in May and June by the Canadians, the French, and the United Nations. In mid-June Canadian diplomat Chester Ronning spoke with North Vietnam officials in Hanoi on peace possibilities, and at the same time French envoy Jean Saintény was travelling to Cambodia and Peking preparatory to going to Hanoi, to deliver Ho Chi Minh a private message from General de Gaulle. It was at this moment (June 15) that *Le Monde* carried an Agence France Presse dispatch from Hanoi stating that diplomatic circles there had started to feel optimistic about the possibilities for negotiations. The Agence also reported that North Vietnam's Premier, Pham Von Dong stated, in the presence of a Soviet-bloc diplomat, that North Vietnam "like France, was an advocate of neutralization." Five days later Secretary General U Thant suggested a three-point program for ending "one of the most barbarous wars in history;" an end to all bombings of North Vietnam; a mutual de-escalation; and negotiations among those "actually fighting" (that is, including the NLF).

For the Johnson administration these peace feelers and ensuing diplomatic activity came during an inopportune period. They began at the height of the Buddhist uprisings against the Ky government in late April and May (and the feelers may have been intended, at least in part, to aggravate this political crisis in South Vietnam). The U.S. response was the same as that observable under similar conditions in the past: intensification of the war, both to offset a deteriorating political situation and to block any possibilities that the diplomatic efforts might bear fruit.

---

[39] *Newsweek*, June 6, 1966, p. 15.

In late May a series of new "hunter-killer" ground operations was launched in South Vietnam by U.S. forces—even while key units of the South Vietnamese army were absent from the battlefield, busily engaged in repressing the Buddhists. Then air raids on North Vietnam were again stepped up, as witnessed by the May 31st attack on Yenbay—the biggest air raid of the war. But the administration's toughest actions came later, at the precise moment when some diplomatic optimism began to issue from Hanoi, in mid-June. On June 18th, just three days after Agence France Presse reported this optimism, President Johnson called a press conference and promised greater levels of American military escalation ("We must continue to raise the cost of aggression at its source"). There was little doubt that the President was referring to intensified bombings of North Vietnam, extending into Hanoi and Haiphong. Heavy bombings of the Hanoi-Haiphong area oil depots began, eleven days after the President's press conference promise.

To repeat: these steps of escalation—intensified hunter-killer operations, the Yenbay raid on May 31 and the Hanoi-Haiphong bombings following June 29—fit into a familiar pattern of Johnsonian action. First, they were a counterweight to renewed governmental instability in Saigon. Second, they undermined all efforts toward the opening of a peaceful dialogue. A report from Hanoi after the Hanoi-Haiphong bombings provided the epitaph to the May-June round. M. Jean Raffaeli of Agence France Presse wrote that the U.S. bombings of the oil depots may have been "an error" politically, because they came at a time when Hanoi's leaders were showing renewed interest in negotiations. M. Raffaeli added that there had been a number of indications to this effect during the month of June.[40]

The only difference between this and the other 1965-66 episodes we have described is that by now the administration's public relations tactics were becoming perfunctory. The President himself, in his June 18th press conference and his June 30th speech at Omaha,[41] scarcely even alluded to the possibility of negotiations.

---

[40] *New York Times*, July 4, 1966.

[41] An "extraordinarily defiant and emotional" speech; *New York Times*, July 3, 1966 (editorial).

Nonetheless, some of the old manipulative devices were still in evidence. To clear the way for escalation, U.S. Undersecretary of State William Bundy flew to Ottawa on June 21st, to confer with Ronning. The information Bundy received was promptly categorized as "pessimistic," although there is evidence that Ronning himself did not share that view.[42] Shortly thereafter, when a State Department spokesman was asked about the latest diplomatic activity, he replied that chances for a positive outcome were slim: "Hanoi's attitude continues to be that expressed last January 24 [1966]." [43] Yet the position taken at that time by Hanoi in Ho Chi Minh's "Letter on Peace Conditions" (to which the spokesman was undoubtedly referring) is that "The four point stand . . . is an expression of the essential provisions of the 1954 Geneva Accords on Vietnam." Since both the four points and the Geneva Accords have been described by Washington as possible bases for discussion, the spokesman's remark seems to offer further proof of unilateral U.S. rejection of all North Vietnamese diplomatic offers short of surrender.

---

[42] The Ronning affair provides another example of administration attempts to involve the Canadians in an unsuccessful U.S. "peace" move, so as to prepare the ground for further escalation. (See Ch. IV, note 23.) In addition to Bundy's "pessimistic" information, Washington officials apparently fed the press another negative report about the Ronning mission—a report published in the *Washington Post,* July 8, 1966. (See *I. F. Stone's Weekly,* July 25, 1966.)

In contrast, on June 22nd (one week before the Hanoi-Haiphong bombings) Canada's Minister of External Affairs, Paul Martin, told the Canadian House of Commons that Ronning had been "well received" in Hanoi and that Canada would continue "the process of patient exploration." On June 26th David Kraslow reported in the *Los Angeles Times* that high U.S. officials in Ottawa agreed that Ronning had opened "a unique and useful" channel to Hanoi: "We want him to keep trying, to keep talking," these officials stated. "Ronning's mission to Hanoi," according to Bernard Fall, "was rapidly touted [in Washington] as a 'total failure,' even though, according to unimpeachable reports, Ronning himself did not see it that way." Fall shares the opinion that Hanoi's actions during May and June "could have been considered a significant step toward a new middle ground." (*New Republic,* July 16, 1966.)

[43] *New York Times,* June 26, 1966.

VI

SUMMARY AND CONCLUSIONS

• It has been firmly established that during the fall of 1964, prior to the escalation of the war by the Johnson administration in February 1965, Hanoi was ready to discuss and negotiate, but the United States twice refused outright. On one occasion it refused even to name its own terms. Washington has claimed that North Vietnam was not ready for "serious talks," but this was never determined by direct contact, and the repeated claim that the escalation was needed to improve our own bargaining position also indicates that only the United States was unwilling to negotiate. A recent book by *Newsweek* White House correspondent Charles Roberts (*LBJ's Inner Circle*, pp. 20-22) reveals, further, that President Johnson had decided to attack North Vietnam back in October 1964, prior to the second negotiation effort by U Thant, and while Johnson was denouncing Barry Goldwater for his propensity to shoot from the hip. The *New York Times* (May 20, 1966) claims that the decision to attack North Vietnam may have been made even earlier than October 1964.

• North Vietnam responded both to President Johnson's April 7, 1965, call for discussions and to the bombing lull of mid-May 1965. Although Hanoi's counter proposals were rejected by Washington as unacceptable, U.S. spokesmen acknowledged in August that these replies were in fact a reasonable starting point for discussions. Such behavior suggests that the failure of the North Vietnamese response to elicit any further diplomatic exchanges was a result of the *absence of any intention to negotiate* on the part of the Johnson administration in the spring and summer of 1965. This is confirmed by a mass of other evidence and by subsequent developments through the late spring of 1966—discussed in the body of this book. They indicate no significant increases in Washington's willingness to grant con-

76

cessions that would make its call for "negotiations" something more than an invitation to surrender.

• The Johnson administration has never felt able to negotiate in Vietnam because *real* negotiations would necessitate political concessions to the National Liberation Front. There is little doubt that the NLF commands more support in South Vietnam than any or all of the cliques of generals supported by the United States in Saigon. It surely commands more popular support than General Ky, who has openly admitted that fact. And even if Ky should outlive his usefulness in the eyes of the United States and should be discarded as was Diem when he proved to be a liability, the United States would undoubtedly find another acceptable anti-Communist military substitute. Though the Johnson administration still supports General Ky, its officials have made it "plain that they supported the government and not any single figure in it. Thus they suggested a willingness to acquiesce in the elevation of another *military leader*" (Max Frankel, *New York Times*, May 21, 1966).

Given the relative political power of the NLF and of the Saigon cliques, free elections and self-determination for the people of South Vietnam are incompatible with the fundamental objective of the United States in South Vietnam, namely, the preservation of an anti-Communist bastion allied with us. (This must be regarded as an underlying "precondition"—without assurance that an "independent" South Vietnam will emerge from the present conflict, Washington has been unready to negotiate.) The same incompatibility explains why the United States cooperated with Diem in refusing to carry out the unifying elections in 1956, as called for by the Geneva Agreements of 1954. To all indications, an "independent" Vietnam would not have survived such elections.

The United States has steadfastly maintained that it will deal only with "governments," and that the NLF can be represented in any conference, but solely as part of a North Vietnamese delegation. This requires the tacit acknowledgement by the NLF that it is simply a tool of Hanoi, which it does not appear to be. The refusal by the United States to deal directly with the NLF, or to concede the possibility of its sharing political power, ignores the political realities of South Vietnam. These are the major

"preconditions" that have consistently stood in the way of a
truce or permanent settlement of the war.

• The refusal of the United States to make any political concessions to the NLF, and its refusal to negotiate, are sometimes
defended on the ground that concessions are not called for when
we are simply resisting "aggression from the North." This is an
Orwellian inversion that stands the truth on its head. The evidence is overwhelming that (a) the rebellion in the South was
mainly a result of indigenous southern opposition to an oppres-
sive, unpopular, totalitarian regime; (b) that support for the
NLF in the South has been considerable, particularly among the
peasantry, and certainly greater than the support given by the
people of South Vietnam to the Saigon cliques sustained by the
United States; and (c) that at each stage in this civil conflict,
the total aid given the NLF by North Vietnam has been a small
fraction of the assistance the United States has provided the
Saigon governments. Furthermore, the refusal by the Diem
government, with Washington approval, to participate in the
peaceful unification of Vietnam by elections in 1956, as called
for by the Geneva Agreements, seriously undermined the moral
and legal basis for any U.S. claims of "aggression from the
North."

The declaration of "aggression from the North" by the United
States in February 1965 was actually an announcement of its
unilateral refusal to accept the loss of a civil war. By denying
the crucial *civil* element of the conflict, the United States could
then justify the unlimited application of force to destroy those
indigenous rebel forces within South Vietnam that had attained
dominant social and political power. The only *real* aggression
in Vietnam, then, is the aerial destruction of North Vietnam and
the massive suppression of the civil war in South Vietnam by the
United States.

• Since negotiations that would recognize the existing distribution of popular support and power in South Vietnam have
always been in conflict with American aims, the call for "discussions" and "negotiations" has had a strictly public relations
function: to provide a deceptive cover for a win policy. The
technique employed in this public relations strategy has been
to call loudly for "unconditional" discussions or negotiations,

while insisting (less vocally) on preconditions that call for the unqualified surrender of all claims by the NLF and North Vietnam.

U.S. preconditions have been made known to the enemy, explicitly and implicitly. North Vietnam now understands that a private language is being employed for public relations effect by the Johnson administration, and that in this language "negotiations" are equated with "cessation of 'aggression'" and with "willingness to surrender." When the enemy has insisted on responding with proposals that might lead to *real* negotiations, the responses have been suppressed, or declared "not encouraging," and sometimes answered with signals like intensified bombings. All these have made clear Washington's intention to discourage any responses other than the awaited willingness to surrender.

Although the "credibility" of the Johnson administration has been increasingly questioned, its public relations strategy has been relatively successful. With the tacit cooperation of most of the communications media, it has persuaded a substantial portion of the American public to accept another Orwellian inversion: that the United States has sincerely pursued negotiations, while the response of the enemy has been entirely negative.

• As we have shown in detail, Hanoi's responses to the peace moves of the Johnson administration have by no means been entirely negative. Throughout 1965, according to Lacouture, "no Washington gesture went unanswered by Hanoi" (*Vietnam Between Two Truces*, p. 282). But North Vietnam's replies have regularly failed to elicit any further American counter-proposals; and the military escalation commonly engaged in by Washington in the midst of its "peace moves" has conveyed a negative picture to North Vietnam (if not to the American public).

Hanoi has been ineffective in its own public relations, partly because of its inability to get a fair hearing in the United States and Britain in particular, but also because it has not been in a position to trumpet any desire to negotiate. A victim of open attack by a powerful foreign aggressor, North Vietnam probably feels that it must avoid signs of weakness—such as would be manifested by an obvious eagerness to negotiate. As the lesser and more vulnerable power, North Vietnam also must be sensitive to the effects of its actions on the morale of its populace. For this reason, since a peace conference would raise domestic hopes for peace, Hanoi cannot involve itself in open talks unless there is a strong possibility of a reasonably successful outcome. (All the more so, since during any conference not preceded by a complete cease fire, the United States could continue to inflict heavy damage upon North Vietnam, with only minor retaliation.)

Furthermore, Hanoi has been in a difficult position as a consequence of the American refusal to deal with the NLF. North Vietnam does not control the NLF, and it cannot negotiate for it. And Hanoi must avoid the stigma of once again selling out the Vietminh forces of the South (as in 1954-1956). In addition, since China has been fearful of a collapse of Vietnamese resistance to American aggression, it appears to have exercised its influence to induce North Vietnam to adhere to a "hard line."

This "hard line" has been an insistence on a prior agreement to a return to the essentials of the Geneva Accords as a precondition to entry into negotiations. The United States also claims to favor a return to the essentials of Geneva; but for it the essentials are the *military* agreements, which the Accords clearly declare to be in no sense a basis of a *political* settlement.

The United States has consistently refused to honor the *political* solution spelled out in the Final Declaration at Geneva, which calls for unifying elections without any qualifications whatsoever. If the Geneva Accords envisaged Vietnam as one country, only temporarily divided, then it also follows that the only "foreign troops" in Vietnam in contravention of the Accords are those of the United States and its allies. In view of the wholesale violations of the Geneva principles of Vietnamese unity, independence, and freedom from use as foreign bases, it is not, after all, a very hard line to insist on an acceptance of these essentials before any negotiations begin. [1]

• The essence of the Johnson policy in Vietnam is escalation to the degree necessary to induce North Vietnam to withdraw support from the NLF, then to crush the NLF by force of arms. Unfortunately, the extent of popular support for the NLF has

---

[1] On the famous third point of Hanoi's preconditions, see Ch. IV, pp. 45-46.

been under-estimated, and the degree to which the Americanization of the war would further isolate the Saigon governments and stiffen Vietnamese resistance has also been miscalculated. Nevertheless, the initial logic of the Johnson policy remains technologically feasible. It now appears, however, that the strength of the enemy and the magnitude of his support in the villages is sufficiently great that the degree of escalation necessary to bring victory will require something approximating genocide. The saturation bombings of hundreds of villages, the deliberate (and acknowledged) destruction of rice crops by chemical means, and the open initiation of a scorched earth policy in the Delta all suggest that the present administration is fully capable of committing genocide, in the absence of domestic or foreign pressures that have not as yet become strong enough to reverse the momentum of the escalation process.

• It is possible that current policy will someday be changed if the economic or political costs of victory come to seem excessive; but such developments have not yet occurred.

If any single lesson can be drawn from the experience of the past two years, it is the need for great scepticism in evaluating the statements of an administration that has shown itself to be unscrupulous in its efforts to manipulate public opinion into accepting plain aggression in the name of "freedom."

THE FAILURE TO HOLD ELECTIONS IN 1956

Article 7 of the Final Declaration at Geneva, July 21, 1954, calls for a political settlement based on "free general elections by secret ballot." It states that "General elections shall be held in July 1956 under the supervision of an international commission composed of representatives of the member states of the International Supervisory Commission, referred to in the agreement on the cessation of hostilities. Consultations will be held on this subject between the competent representative authorities of the two zones from 20 July onwards."

Although the Article is reasonably straightforward, Ngo Dinh Diem announced on July 16, 1955 (with the support of the United States) that his government would refuse to participate in the scheduled conferences or in the free elections called for in 1956. The Hanoi government protested and at least seven times (through 1960) it attempted to have the elections carried out and to have the French discharge their obligations as signers and guarantors of the Geneva Accords in the southern area.[1]

As is amply evident, the failure to carry through the unifying elections seriously undermines the legal and moral positions of both Saigon and Washington. Refusal to permit the employment of the peaceful mechanism for a political settlement called for by the Geneva Accords—an internationally supervised election—

---

[1] Authoritative accounts of these events can be found in George Kahin and John Lewis, "The United States in Vietnam," *Bulletin of the Atomic Scientists*, June 1965, esp. pp. 29-31, and Philippe Devillers, "The Struggle for the Unification of Vietnam," *China Quarterly*, Jan.-March 1962, esp. pp. 6-11 (reprinted in Marvin Gettleman, ed., *Vietnam*). See also "North Vietnam Premier Renews Proposal to South for Conference on Unification," ("It was the third time in three years that he had made such a proposal") Tillman Durdin, *New York Times*, July 21, 1957, and "North Vietnam Asks Parley with South," *New York Times*, Dec. 27, 1958.

At least until 1960 North Vietnam rather closely observed the Geneva Accords; certainly it adhered to them more closely than did calls into question the validity of the American charge of North Vietnamese "aggression." (In Appendix 3 we show that the charge is an Orwellian inversion in virtually every substantive aspect).

Why then, in view of their subsequent failure at implementation, did the Western powers agree to the inclusion of the proviso for unifying elections? In his book, *Vietnam Divided,* B. S. N. Murti, Deputy Secretary-General of the International Control Commission from 1954 to 1957, suggests the following explanation: "Most probably the precarious military situation at the time of the Geneva Conference in Indo-China and the refusal of the North Vietnamese Government to agree to a truce without a political settlement must have forced them to accept elections, without being very serious about their commitments. . . . The very fact that the Western powers wanted no political settlement and suggested a ten year time-limit after cease-fire for general elections, then came down to five years and finally were forced to agree to two years for political settlement because of the military situation at that time, makes one wonder whether they were ever serious about a political settlement in Vietnam. This doubt was substantiated by subsequent events and attitudes taken by them." (p. 179-180.)

Murti then goes on to point out that "As early as January, 1955, the *Economist* in an editorial stated that the American policy since Geneva had clearly been directed toward strengthening the Saigon regime and the aid given was obviously not meant to provide a free gift for the Viet Minh at the expense of the American tax-payer. It presumed that the only intelligible aim of the American policy was to give the Southern

---

the Diem government. See Jean Lacouture, *Vietnam Between Two Truces,* pp. 34-35, and Gettleman, *op. cit.,* pp. 160-67.

Perhaps the best summary of where the onus for destroying the Geneva Accords must lie is from the unanimous finding of the International Control Commission (executors of the Geneva Accords), in its *Sixth Interim Report* (Jan. 1957): "The degree of cooperation given to the Commission by the two parties has not been the same. While the Commission has experienced difficulties in North Vietnam, the major part of its difficulties has arisen in South Vietnam."

Government the best possible chance of survival on as permanent a basis as that of South Korea. According to Mr. C. L. Sulzberger, the *New York Times* columnist [March 12, 1955], all Vietnam elections 'really will never be held. . . . The non-Communist South cannot afford the slightest risk of defeat. Nobody likes to talk about this but when the time comes to admit it arrives, a grave crisis must inevitably develop'."

How has the U.S. government explained the failure to carry out the 1956 elections? First, it has offered the theory that the election proviso of the Geneva Agreements was based upon a Communist plot. In the State Department's White Paper of December 1961, *A Threat to the Peace,* it is stated that "It was the Communists' calculation that nationwide elections scheduled in the Accords for 1956 would turn all of South Vietnam over to them . . . The authorities in South Vietnam refused to fall into this well-laid trap." Of course such an insidious trap as unification by free elections (as "scheduled in the Accords for 1956") must not be permitted! It should be obvious that this "explanation," and the failure to urge that the elections be carried out in 1956, contradict the proclaimed interest of the United States in "self determination" and violate the 1954 pledge "to seek to achieve unity through free elections . . . in the case of nations divided against their will." Furthermore, if the United States will not permit genuine elections in Vietnam so long as it seems probable that the Communists will win, it is rather hypocritical to pontificate, à la Rusk and Goldberg, about the inability of the Communists to win free elections.

A second reason sometimes advanced for the failure to hold free elections in 1956 is that with the Communists in control of the North, it is impossible to hold *really* free elections. This is argued on two grounds: (a) that the Communists are not *willing* to hold genuinely free elections; and (b) that brain-washing and threats of reprisals by the Communists make free elections impossible. In general, this position suggests bad faith on the part of the participants in the Geneva Conference and those with the legal and moral obligation to carry through the Agreements; for Communist "control" of the North was an essential feature of the *preliminary* arrangements, which were to be *followed* by free elections.

The first argument was presented by Secretary Rusk in his February 1966 testimony before the Senate Foreign Relations Committee: "And then it worked out so that North Vietnam was not interested at all in holding anything like genuinely free elections." This is a particularly flagrant misrepresentation. The North Vietnamese requested time and again that the conferences to arrange for the election be held, but on every occasion they were rebuffed by Diem. What makes Mr. Rusk's remark so patently false is the fact that Diem, with American backing, was unwilling even to attend the preliminary conferences and *to state the electoral and supervisory conditions under which he would permit free elections to be held.* Clearly, the Diem government and its American backer were not interested in any free elections —and it is also evident that the North Vietnamese called for the implementation of the election proviso of the Geneva Accords, and their bluff (if bluff it was) was never called.

As regards the contention that Communist brain-washing would render really free elections impossible: this argument overlooks the offsetting consideration that severe Communist intimidation and oppression would undoubtedly generate hostility that could be turned to the other side's advantage in a free election. For example, it has been argued that in 1955-56 the Vietminh launched a "reign of terror" in the North, a reflection of which was the "small peasant revolt of Nghé An crushed in November 1956 . . . [and] highly exploited by Diem's propaganda machine." [2] There is little doubt that repression of dissident elements was taking place in the North. The Nghé An episode has often been referred to by supporters of the U.S. intervention in Vietnam to justify Diem's refusal to hold the elections. But it, and nearly all other reports of repression in the North, *followed* Diem's election refusal by sixteen months or more. Furthermore, if the unrest and resentment in the North were so widespread after these repressions, why was the Diem government unwilling to go to elections in which the population of the North could express its dissatisfaction? All that would have been required for electoral victory was an adequate system of secret balloting and supervision. But, as noted above, Diem was un-

---

[2] Devillers, *op. cit.*, p. 10.

willing even to specify the conditions under which he would participate in the election.

Although the Diem government and its supporters made much of the lack of democratic freedoms in the North as an obstacle to unifying elections, these protestations coincided with the rapid organization of a police state in South Vietnam that permitted "no independent political activity" in the South during its decade of existence (in the words of U. Alexis Johnson, former U. S. Deputy Ambassador to South Vietnam). It is also ironic that while the Diem regime refused to have anything to do with unifying elections, Hanoi went to considerable lengths to spell out electoral conditions that would be acceptable to it. In two letters published in the North Vietnamese newspaper *Nhan Dan,* on November 17, 1955 and February 25, 1956, Ho Chi Minh himself gave a detailed specification of Hanoi's conception of appropriate electoral requirements. (These conditions were, of course, vastly more democratic than those normally prevailing within either North *or* South Vietnam.) As quoted by B. S. N. Murti (*Vietnam Divided,* p. 187), Ho stipulated the following:

"Free Elections: All the Vietnamese citizens, males or female above 18 years old, regardless of class, nationality, religion, political affiliation, have the right to participate in the elections, to vote freely for the persons in whom they have confidence.

"Free Candidature: All Vietnamese citizens, male and female above 21 years old, also with the above-mentioned non-restriction clauses, have the right to stand for elections.

"Free Canvass: All Vietnamese citizens, whether from the North or the South, have the right to canvass freely throughout the country through conference, leaflets, press, etc. The Government of the North and the authorities of the South should ensure the liberty and the security for all citizens during their activities for elections.

"Method of Voting: Totally equal, secret and direct. In short, the Vietnamese people and the Government of the Democratic Republic of Vietnam shall ensure complete freedom and democracy to the nation-wide elections (as provided in the Geneva Agreement)."

According to Murti, "The second letter [by Ho Chi Minh]

proposed a method by which the Western countries could determine which part of Vietnam had democratic freedoms. According to this, the Democratic Republic Government offered to allow any number of representatives of the South to campaign in the North and the Democratic Republic would guarantee their complete security and the right to campaign freely their electoral propaganda provided their own representatives were allowed to do the same in the South." (Pp. 187-188).

The Western powers tried to persuade Diem at least to go through with the form of consultation with the North, to avoid embarrassing them. "Britain and France," says Murti, "tried to clarify the difference between holding elections and merely talking about them which was all that Diem was being asked to do at that stage. They made it clear to Diem that in opening talks with the Viet Minh, he would not be committing himself to anything irrevocable. They also felt that talks would be evidence of their adherence to the accords and allow postponement of a final decision until the South was stronger and politically better organized." But, according to Murti, "None of these assurances could convince South Vietnam and persuade them to start consultations with the North."

A final reason given for the failure to hold the unifying elections is that since neither the United States nor South Vietnam signed the Geneva Accords, neither can be said to have been bound by them (or to have any responsibility for enforcing them).[3] By this logic, only North Vietnam can violate the Accords! But the authors of the Geneva Agreements intended that the unifying elections be carried out in 1956 as the final political settlement in Vietnam; and the United States as the successor power to France had a moral and legal obligation to see that such elec-

---

[3] At Geneva on July 21, 1954, U.S. Undersecretary of State Walter Bedell Smith stated that the United States would "refrain from the threat or use of force to disturb" the Geneva Agreements, and "would view any renewal of the aggression in violation of the aforesaid Agreements with grave concern and as seriously threatening international peace and security." It therefore appears (as Secretary Rusk said; see Ch. II, note 2) that Smith did put the United States on record as recognizing the legal sanctity of the Geneva Agreements—both the formal agreements (signed only by France and the Vietminh) and the Final Declaration (unsigned).

tions were carried out,[*] particularly in view of Washington's pledge to seek unity via free elections for nations divided against the will of the populace. Instead, the United States collaborated with Saigon in a clear violation of this commitment (and our "word of honor").

---

[*]Pointing out that the French "washed their hands" of the Geneva Agreements just a few months before the time-limit prescribed for general elections, B. S. N. Murti goes on to say that "This contingency was visualized at the Geneva Conference and a provision was incorporated in the cease-fire agreement according to which 'the signatories of the present agreement *and their successors in their functions* shall be responsible for ensuring the observance and enforcement of the terms and provisions thereof'." (*Vietnam Divided*, Bombay, 1964, pp. 179-80.)

APPENDIX 2

INDEPENDENCE

As American foreign policy has moved toward the open use of military power to dominate other states, the employment of Orwellian language has become more frequent. Words with emotionally satisfying (or repellent) qualities are increasingly employed to describe their precise opposites. Nowhere is this more in evidence than in the claim by President Johnson and Secretary Rusk that the goal of American policy in Southeast Asia is the preservation of "independent" states.[1]

If the Johnsonian use of this term is examined closely, it will be seen that "dependent" countries are exclusively those in the Communist bloc or those affiliated with them. Conversely, if a country is non-Communist but economically, militarily, or diplomatically influenced by the United States to any substantial degree, it is described as "independent." For instance, South Korea, with over 60,000 American troops on its soil, a standing army of 600,000 paid and equipped chiefly with U.S. funds, and a dictatorship heavily dependent on our aid, continues to be designated an "independent" country. North Korea, with no Chinese or Russian troops known to be within its borders, with a much smaller standing army, and with vastly greater success in unifying the country for the task of national reconstruction,[2] is a "dependency" or "satellite."

Similar Orwellian language was employed in 1951 by the then Assistant Secretary of State Dean Rusk, in explaining U.S. support for Chiang Kai-Shek and opposition to Red China, on the ground of "the historic demand [of the Chinese people] for in-

---

[1] It is also evident in other usages. See especially the use of the word "aggression" in Ch. II, note 5, and in Appendix 3; the use of the word "freedom" in Ch. II; and the Johnsonian concept of "negotiations," discussed throughout the text.

[2] Joan Robinson, "North Korea," in *Collected Economic Papers*, Vol. III (Blackwell, 1966).

89

dependence from foreign control." [3] Mainland China was depicted by Rusk as a "colony" of the Soviet Union, in contrast with the "independent" government of Taiwan. As Leonard Liggio has pointed out, however, "Since no country in the world has shown more independence from foreign control than has mainland China, and since American hostility to Peking has increased proportionately to that independence, one can hardly blame world opinion for suspecting Washington of seeking to arrange the dependence of the mainland on the United States." [4]

To apply an objective standard of independence to the countries in the Southeast Asian and Chinese orbit, it is necessary to assess the degree of influence on their governments exercised by *any* outsiders. One index of the probable dependence of a government on an external power is its attitude toward the presence of foreign troops within its boundaries. Foreign troops may be requested by a truly independent government whose survival is threatened by real aggression. But since alien military forces pose a threat of control by the supporting power, they will be employed reluctantly and as a last resort. On the other hand, foreign troops may be the only basis of domination by adventurers (usually military) without any internal support. [5]

A further index of independence is the degree to which a government's budget is accounted for by subventions provided by a foreign power. Where such assistance is substantial it conveys political leverage, implies considerable influence, and opens the door to outright control.

According to these criteria, the principal allies of the United States in the Southeast Asia—China area are its least independ-

---

[3] *Hearings of Joint Senate Committee*, May 1951, pp. 3191-2.

[4] "Korea—Then and Now," *Viet-Report*, Nov.-Dec. 1965.

[5] Of course, once control begins to slip from the hands of such military adventurers, the country in question begins to become less "independent" from the standpoint of the dominant external power. Therefore, Buddhist agitation against the Saigon military junta is to be deplored: "American officials suggest that the strategy and aims of [leading Buddhist] Thich Tri Quang are basically incompatible with the interests of the United States in Vietnam . . . and they do not feel that any government controlled by Thich Tri Quang *would be amenable to American influence*." (Neil Sheehan, *New York Times*, April 11, 1966.)

ent countries, varying from those strongly subject to U.S. influence to virtual puppet regimes. China and Cambodia have no foreign troops within their borders, receive little or no outside military or economic aid, and both appear to be highly sensitive to threats to their national sovereignty. Even more interesting is North Vietnam, which is often explicitly or implicitly suggested to be a Chinese puppet. There are still no Chinese troops reported in North Vietnam. Seymour Topping recently reported from Hong Kong that "the North Vietnamese want the armies of their Chinese Communist allies to stay at home if possible. Leaders in Hanoi have not allowed their Communist ideology to erase the Vietnamese memory of a thousand years of Chinese domination." [6] Significantly, William P. Bundy was quoted in February 1966 to the effect that North Vietnam "can still make its own decisions" despite Communist Chinese influence. And although there are no statistics available on the amount of material assistance received by North Vietnam from the Chinese, it is interesting that Mr. Bundy also acknowledged that Hanoi was still "seeking to balance the assistance that it receives from the Chinese Communists and the assistance it receives from the Soviet Union." [7]

More recently it was reported that there has been a deterioration of relations between Peking and Hanoi, attributed by some analysts "to the stubborn refusal of the Hanoi leaders to line up with Peking against the Soviet Union. . . . Peking is not concealing its annoyance at the praise lavished on the Kremlin hierarchy by the North Vietnamese delegation to the 23d Congress of the Soviet Communist party in Moscow last month." [8] This is not the behavior of a puppet, and it confirms substantial

[6] "China Tone on Vietnam Increasingly Ominous," *New York Times*, Jan. 30, 1966. See also Topping's description of North Vietnam's "independent foreign policy" (conceded as such by American officials), *New York Times*, May 29, 1966.

[7] "William Bundy Says Hanoi Is Not Under Peking Thumb," U.P.I. report in *New York Times*, Feb. 9, 1966.

[8] Seymour Topping, "Peking is Cooler to Hanoi Leaders," *New York Times*, April 30, 1966. The North Vietnamese attended this conference despite the fact that China chose to boycott it.

evidence that North Vietnam has been and hopes to remain a
distinctly independent albeit friendly neighbor of China.

Even the hard-pressed NLF is by no means a simple dependent
of a "foreign" power (in this case, North Vietnam). There is
good reason to believe that North Vietnam participation in the
conflict in the South was a direct result of pressure from former
Vietminh resistants in the South, rather than a consequence of
northern initiative.[9] The rebels in the South have also been far
less dependent on external aid than the Saigon governments, a
factor making for greater autonomy. Moreover, it is difficult to
reconcile the conception of the NLF as an "arm of Hanoi" with
the fact that the Johnson administration is apparently quite
uncertain that the North Vietnamese government could enforce
a settlement in South Vietnam even if it so desired.[10]

Recent relations between the NLF and Hanoi are described
by the French reporter and scholar Jean Lacouture in these
words:

"Today it is clear that the NLF leaders are closely linked to
Hanoi, on which they depend for much of their supplies and arms.
But anyone concerned with a peaceful settlement in Vietnam
should be aware of both the local origins of the Front and its
strong persisting regionalism—its attachments to the milieux,
traditions, economy and countryside of the South which give it
fundamental autonomy . . .

"[Why doesn't Ho play Lyndon Johnson's game of 'discussion'?] But perhaps they [the North Vietnamese] were not in a
position to negotiate at all. If we look back over the history of
the NLF we find support for the view that Hanoi is not able to
speak for the Front. First for psychological reasons: The published program of the NLF expressly mentions the possibility of an
independent South Vietnam; and it looks forward to forming an
alliance with Laos and Cambodia only. Thus it seems most unlikely that the Front would consider itself adequately represented
by the Northern government. Finally, there may be a purely
practical reason. Combat conditions in the South are such that
it is by no means certain that a decision or an agreement even

---

[9] See Appendix 3.   [10] See Ch. III, note 6.

if approved by the NLF would be supported by all the fighters in the field." [11]

The contrast with South Korea, Taiwan, Thailand, and the Saigon government of South Vietnam could hardly be more marked. Each of these governments has permitted the construction of major U.S. military facilities on its territory; and the number of American military personnel currently in these countries is considerable: Korea, 60,000; Taiwan, 5,000; Thailand, 26,000; and South Vietnam, 285,000 (and growing rapidly). Each of these governments has also been indebted to the United States for economic and military aid amounting to substantial portions of the total national budget. [12]

Another feature of the "independent" governments that support American policy in Asia is that they are all military dictatorships, with little reformist zeal (although they exist in countries having pressing economic and social problems) and limited popular support. This last consideration may explain both why these members of the "free world" never hold free elections and why they permit the massive intrusion of a foreign military establishment: if one is incapable of winning mass domestic support, subordination to a foreign power may be the only means of preserving some vestige of minority power.

Here we have in sharp focus what we may call the "Johnson model" for external domination: an alliance with the military establishment (and rightist elite), which may be encouraged to overthrow a constitutional government (as in Brazil), or aided in obstructing the return of constitutionalism (as in the Dominican Republic). In return, it receives the support necessary to preserve itself in power, so long as it can be counted on to carry out certain essentials—accommodating American investors and subordinating its foreign policy to that of the United States. [13] The full cooperation of the Branco dictatorship

---

[11] *New York Review of Books*, March 3, 1966.

[12] Robert Guillain was told recently by an American official in Saigon that the United States is furnishing approximately 80 per cent of South Vietnam's national budget expenditures; "Vietnam Recolonized," *Le Monde*, May 26-June 1, 1966.

[13] Military assistance pacts which the United States has signed with many countries "are designed, above all, to draw the Latin Ameri-

of Brazil in the U. S. venture in the Dominican Republic in
April 1965 is indicative of the nature of the newly discovered
"independence" of Brazil. The "almost desperate desire" of the
Saigon cliques not to be pushed into negotiations "until they
are more able to compete politically with the Vietnamese Communists" also reflects the "independence" of the Johnson model
of government.[14]

In his speech of February 23, 1966, President Johnson stated
that "Washington will not impose upon the people of South
Vietnam a government not of their own choice." As in the case
of so many of our leaders' statements, conversion into its opposite
places one much closer to the truth. From the hand-picking of
Diem and his imposition on the South Vietnamese, up to the
commitments to General Ky (who has frankly acknowledged
his incapacity to maintain power under conditions of free electoral choice) the role of the United States has been one of
aiding, and more recently imposing, minority governments con-
ceived to be amenable to our own interests.

American power and influence in Saigon have become so great
that when Mr. Cabot Lodge stated before a Congressional committee that the United States would not leave South Vietnam
even if the government of that country asked us to do so, he
caused hardly a ripple in South Vietnam. Lodge's statement,
never denied outright, was shortly thereafter amplified by an
anonymous "high official" in Washington who explained the

---

can officer corps, which exercise great influence over the political
scene in most of the republics, closer to the United States, in the
hope that they will exclude Soviet influence, give the United States
their support, maintain political stability, ensure continued access
to strategic raw materials, and provide rights to the use of bases."
Edwin Lieuwin, *Arms and Politics in Latin America* (New York,
1960), p. 226.

[14] The question of independence has also been of importance in
Greece. The overthrow of the Papandreou government in July
1965 was linked to its restiveness at subordination to the United
States—a subordination that had been quite acceptable to the mon-
archy-military group that dominated Greek affairs following the
civil war of 1947-48. Andreas Papandreou revealed publicly that
the intelligence agency of the Greek government had been the re-
cipient of an annual subsidy from the American Central Intelligence Agency, to the amount of $400,000. The refusal of the Papan-

Lodge remark as meaning that the United States would not withdraw if asked to do so "by a left-wing or even neutralist government that, in the U. S. view, did not reflect the true feelings of the South Vietnamese people *or military leaders*." [15]

Washington's conception of the "free choice" of the South Vietnamese people, in short, has much in common with the language of imperialist domination. Its open employment by officials of the United States bespeaks volumes as to who is *really* trying to "impose a government on the people of South Vietnam."

dreou government to accept the U.S. solution to the Cyprus conflict, and hints that the Prime Minister was contemplating a trip to Moscow, were received with consternation by Washington—for the United States had been used to getting its way in "independent" Greece. See the series on Greece by Eric Rouleau in *Le Monde*: Aug. 19-25, Sept. 23-29, Sept. 30-Oct. 6, and Oct. 7-13, 1965.

[15] *New York Times*, Aug. 13, 1965.

AGGRESSION BY WHOM?

The primary rationalization for U. S. military intervention in Vietnam is to protect the government and people of South Vietnam against "aggression" from the North. In his press conference of June 18, 1966, President Johnson used the words "aggressor" and "aggression" ten different times in defending his intention to escalate the war again. This alleged aggression makes it possible to justify whatever level of destruction is imposed upon Vietnam in the name of a "principle," with appropriate references to Hitler, Munich, and so forth.

Of course, the other side of the coin is that if the American charge of aggression cannot be sustained, then the United States itself would be engaging in aggression against North Vietnam and in an attempt to suppress an internal upheaval in South Vietnam.

The Role of China

It is not clear who the "Hitler" is in the present case. Secretaries Rusk and MacNamara have compared Mao Tse-Tung with Hitler—an insult to General Ky, who has proclaimed Hitler *his* only hero[1]—but Chinese aggression in Vietnam has been of an extraordinary character. No Chinese troops have been reported in Vietnam up to now (August 1966). And no evidence at all has been advanced to show that China either controls North Vietnamese foreign policy or had any major influence on Hanoi's 1960 decision to give active support to the insurgency in South Vietnam. In Appendix 2 and elsewhere in this book, we cite some of the large body of evidence indicating that the North Vietnamese Communists are strongly nationalistic and jealously protective of their autonomy against their powerful Chinese neighbor. Further, we have also shown[2] that there is

[1] See Ch. II, note 13.

[2] See Appendix 2 and Ch. III, note 6.

good reason to question whether the North Vietnamese (let alone the Chinese) have decisive influence over the NLF forces in South Vietnam.

The Chinese would obviously prefer a weak and friendly power in Vietnam to a U. S.-sustained regime, and China has declared its support for the insurgency. But the NLF and much of the Vietnamese peasantry are not fighting to the death for Chinese interests. They are dedicated to their own cause, which in this instance overlaps that of the Chinese. In the absence of any evidence that China initiated, directly participated in, or has exercised decisive influence over those doing the fighting in Vietnam, Chinese "aggression" in Vietnam must be regarded as a product of anti-Communist metaphysics.

Chinese behavior has actually been quite cautious.[3] Because of that, American officials have laid much stress on China's bellicose language and its declaration that Vietnam is a "test case" of wars of national liberation. Yet—as American spokesmen have pointed out on occasions when convenient—deeds and capabilities are considerably more important than words. And in addition, the Chinese *words* themselves have been seriously misrepresented. The Chinese have consistently called for *others* to rise up and throw off the shackles of imperialism; and they have placed great emphasis on the need for "self-reliance" and a domestic mass-base for a successful national liberation movement.[4] Chinese support is de-emphasized,[5] and there is

---

[3] So cautious, in fact, that in its military escalations the United States has counted heavily upon Chinese prudence and restraint. American officials have gone even further than their British and French counterparts in minimizing the danger of Chinese intervention in Vietnam. It is indeed a bizarre sort of "Chinese aggression" that permits large-scale military activity by a foreign power on its own rimlands!

[4] "The liberation of the masses," according to Marshal Lin Piao, "is accomplished by the masses themselves—this is the basic principle of Marxism-Leninism. Revolution or peoples' war in any country is the business of the masses in that country and should be carried out primarily by their own efforts; there is no other way . . . In order to make a revolution and to fight a peoples' war and be

nothing to indicate a determination to control these national
liberation movements, or to dominate other countries in their
area, let alone in the western hemisphere. We have not been
able to find any Chinese statement so directly threatening to
a potential enemy, or any other country, and so clearly expressing
an intention to dominate Asia, as that made by U. S. Assistant
Secretary of State for Far Eastern Affairs, Walter S. Robertson,
in January 1954.[6]

It has also been emphasized that the Chinese have declared
Vietnam to be a "test case" of wars of national liberation; they
have "challenged" us. But this fails to prove any substantial
Chinese participation in the Vietnam conflict. Moreover, in a
rational world it might be assumed that a test chosen by an
enemy would be something to avoid. The test in South Vietnam
is disadvantageous to the United States—it is at a great distance,
and the war of national liberation *has* a mass base in that country.
If the leaders of the United States choose to accept this test on

---

victorious, it is imperative to adhere to a policy of self-reliance, rely
on the strength of the masses in one's own country and prepare to
carry on the fight independently even when all material aid from
outside is cut off." *Long Live the Victory of the Peoples' War*
(Peking, 1965), pp. 38, 41.

[5] "The peoples of the world invariably support each other in their
struggles against imperialism and its lackeys. Those countries
which have won victory are duty bound to support and aid the peoples which have not yet done so. Nevertheless, foreign aid can
only play a supplementary role . . . If one does not operate by one's
own efforts, does not independently ponder and solve the problems
of the revolution in one's own country and does not rely on the
strength of the masses, but leans wholly on foreign aid—even
though this be aid from socialist countries which persist in revolution—no victory can be won, or be consolidated even if it is won."
(*Ibid.*, pp. 41-42.)

Instead of being a "Chinese *Mein Kampf*" and blueprint for world
conquest, the Lin Piao statement appears instead to be more a
rationalization for Chinese *non-action* in revolutionary situations.
See Donald Zagoria, "China's Crisis of Foreign Policy," *New York
Times*, May 1, 1966.

[6] *Representative Frederick R. Coudert:* "Did I correctly understand you to say that the heart of the present policy toward China
and Formosa is that there be kept alive a constant threat of mili-

the very borders of China, it is they who challenge and provoke, and with deeds, not words.

The Roles of North Vietnam and the United States

Is North Vietnam an aggressor against the independent state of South Vietnam, or was the conflict essentially a civil war prior to the 1965 escalation by the United States?

Any answer must take into consideration the following questions: Is South Vietnam an independent state that can be aggressed against by North Vietnam? Did the insurgency in South Vietnam originate among the indigenous population or was it brought in from the outside? If the conflict was originally southern but was subsequently enlarged by U.S. and North Vietnamese intervention, who started this expansion? What has been the relative degree of dependence of the participants on external sources of manpower and material? What is the relative degree of external control over the NLF on the one hand, and the Saigon governments on the other? What is the comparative extent of indigenous support for the NLF and the Saigon governments?

We shall discuss each of these questions in turn and then attempt to draw a balance.

Is South Vietnam an independent state that can be aggressed against by North Vietnam?

It has previously been noted[7] that the 1954 political settlement at Geneva called for free, unifying elections to be held

---

tary action vis-a-vis Red China in the hope that at some point there will be an internal breakdown?"

Robertson: "Yes, sir. That is my conception."

Coudert: "In other words, a cold war waged under the leadership of the United States, with constant threat of attack against Red China, led by Formosa and other Far Eastern groups, and militarily backed by the United States?"

Robertson: "Yes . . ."

Coudert: "Fundamentally, does that mean that the United States is undertaking to maintain for an indefinite period of years American dominance in the Far East?"

Robertson: "Yes. Exactly." (Hearings before the House Committee on Appropriations, Jan. 26, 1954, pp. 125, 127.)

[7] See Appendix 1.

in 1956, and that these elections were openly blocked by the
action of the South Vietnamese and U. S. governments. Hence,
the legal "independence" of South Vietnam is a consequence of a
violation of the letter and spirit of the Geneva Accords. George
Kahin and John Lewis have posed the following relevant question: "When a military struggle for power ends on the agreed
condition that the competition will be transferred to the political
level, can the side which violates the agreed conditions legiti-
mately expect that the military struggle will not be resumed?"[8]
More explicitly, if the military struggle is resumed, does the side
which violated the agreed conditions have the "clean hands"
that might justify the accusation of "aggression"?

*Did the insurgency in South Vietnam originate within its
borders or from the outside?*

Most independent authorities conclude that the fighting in
South Vietnam was initiated in the South. They generally agree
that it was produced by a viciously repressive regime that was
unable or unwilling to cope with fundamental economic and
social problems.

"It was thus by its *home* policy," Philippe Devillers states,
"that the government of the South finally destroyed the confidence of the population, which it had won during the early years,
and practically drove them into revolt and desperation. . . .
[Moreover], the insurrection existed before the Communists
decided to take part, and . . . they were simply forced to join in.
And even among the Communists, the initiative did not originate
from Hanoi, but from the grass roots, where the people were
literally driven by Diem to take up arms in self defense."[9]

According to Jean Lacouture "a careful study of the history of
South Vietnam over the last ten years will show that from 1956
onward, strong resistance groups, the surviving members of po-
litical-religious sects crushed by Diem, were in active opposition

[8] "The United States in Vietnam," *Bulletin of the Atomic Scientists,* June 1965, p. 31.

[9] "The Struggle for the Unification of Vietnam," *China Quarterly,*
Jan.-March 1962, reprinted in Gettleman, *op. cit.*

to the regime in the South; they were in fact already called
'Vietcong' by the Diem regime at that time. Furthermore, this
essentially nationalist dissident movement gained additional
support as a result of the rural discontent which led Diem to
suppress the elected municipal councils in 1957; it spread further after the promulgation of the terrible law of 1959 which
prescribed the death penalty for all 'accomplices of Communists'
—and Communism comes cheap in South Vietnam. At this time
the resistance was composed of nothing more than Southern
groups organized in self-defense against Diem. Hanoi had made
no connection with them. The North Vietnamese did not begin
to exploit this situation and infiltrate agents until 1959; and it
was only after pressure from a Southern congress of 'former
Vietminh resistants' in March of 1960 that they prepared to
intervene."[10]

While tending to differ with some experts on the question
of North Vietnamese "control" over the NLF after 1960, Bernard
Fall supports the views of Devillers and Lacouture on the origins
of the conflict:

"It is axiomatic in the field of revolutionary warfare that the
potential insurgent takes his source of power from a population
which (in the words of the U. S. Army manual of *Counterguerilla
Operations* [FM 31-16]) has 'become discontented with existing
conditions which cannot be changed by peaceful and legal means."
That is close to a perfect definition of what was to happen in
South Vietnam *not*—contrary to some later appraisals—after
1960 or 1961, but starting in 1956. . . . Communists cadres
will exploit occasions when they arise, but they are incapable
of 'creating' a revolution from scratch. It is Diem who created
the movement of discontent in South Vietnam. North Vietnam
and the Vietcong fed on it. . . . [Thus] neither North Vietnam
nor the [U. S.] State Department explain the existence of
guerrilla warfare in South Vietnam in the years from 1956 to
1960. That such guerrilla warfare indeed existed can be fully
documented and was in fact so documented by this writer as
early as 1958 [in *Pacific Affairs*, Sept. 1958]. On May 6, 1959
the Diem regime passed law 10/59, which provided for a system

---

[10] *New York Review of Books*, March 3, 1966.

of drumhead courts capable of handing out death sentences for
even trivial offenses. Thus, *all* South Vietnamese opposition—
whether Communist or not—had to become subversive, and
did."[11]

Furthermore, Fall points out—as do Lacouture and Devillers
—that Hanoi's celebrated statement of support for the NLF in
December 1960 was in fact an indication of how its hand was
being forced by events in the South: "In the typically conserva-
tive fashion of Communist regimes subsequent to the Greek and
Filipino disappointments, Hanoi still hesitated to commit itself
to the side of the guerrillas." [12]

With reference to the third congress of the North Vietnamese
Communist Party at Hanoi in September 1960, Lacouture states:
"Here, for the first time, Northern Communist leaders indi-

---

[11] "Vietnam: The New Korea," *Current History*, Feb. 1966, pp.
88, 117 (emphasis in original).

For similar views on the origins of the conflict, all rejecting
the "aggression from the North" thesis, see: Malcolm Browne,
The New Face of War (Indianapolis, 1965), esp. pp. 24, 146, and
Ch. 12; Joseph Kraft, "Understanding the Vietcong," *New York
Review of Books*, Aug. 5, 1965; Tran Van Dinh (former South
Vietnamese representative to UNESCO), "Le déclin des mythes au
Vietnam du Sud," *Le Monde*, July 29-Aug. 4, 1965; Murti, *op. cit.*,
preface and pp. 178, 196-97; and Richard Starnes, especially his
columns of Jan. 4, 1965 and Jan. 21, 1966, carried in Scripps-Howard
newspapers.

In addition to Starnes, other American correspondents with
Vietnam experience agree on the southern origins of the war.
Contrasting the Korean war with Vietnam, American Broadcasting
Company reporter Lou Chioffi stated that in South Vietnam . . .
"there's been no real armed aggression from the North or anywhere else. It's an insurrection." (ABC-TV, Jan. 15, 1966.) A television panel on Aug. 1, 1966, devoted to a discussion of U.S. news
policies in Saigon, included Dean Brelis of N.B.C., Charles Mohr
of the *New York Times*, Jack Foisie of the *Los Angeles Times*, and
Malcolm Browne, former A.P. reporter. Browne stated that the
administration, and "particularly Secretary McNamara, have deliberately misled American opinion." An example, he said, is "the
continual harping on the North Vietnamese aggression." Browne
asserted that the war was basically a civil war; the other three
correspondents agreed. (*New York Times*, Aug. 2, 1966.)

[12] *Ibid.*, p. 118.

cated an interest in what was going on in South Vietnam. The goal of 'liberating South Vietnam from American imperialism' was placed on the same footing as the goal of building socialism in the North . . . however, it must be emphasized that the Hanoi leaders did not make this shift—still a cautious one at that—on their own, but rather in response to the pressure of militants in the South who criticized the rather indifferent attitude of their Northern comrades toward the repressive measures of the Saigon authorities." [13]

In sum, whatever the relative timing and degree of North Vietnamese and U. S. intervention, the evidence is strong that the fighting in South Vietnam had southern origins and was not initiated from the outside. [14]

If the conflict in South Vietnam was originally southern, but was eventually enlarged by intervention on the part of North Vietnam and the United States, who initiated this expansion in the conflict?

Although this is one of those "chicken and egg" questions on which a definitive judgment is somewhat hazardous, the balance of evidence seems to us sufficiently strong to support the conclusion that the United States-Diem alliance was mainly responsible for the extension of the conflict. This was not a consequence of any moral superiority on the part of the Vietminh forces—it followed from their interest in preserving the Geneva Accords and in not providing any excuse for violation of the election proviso, whose implementation they expected to redound to their benefit. The Vietminh's emphasis on a political solution was acknowledged in the State Department's White Paper *A Threat to the Peace*: "The primary focus of the Communists' activity during the post-Geneva period was on political action—

---

[13] *New Republic*, March 6, 1965.

[14] Secretary McNamara confuted the alleged civil war character of the conflict in South Vietnam by asserting before the Senate Foreign Relations Committee (April 20, 1966) that "In 1960, in Hanoi, at the first conference of the Laodong Party, the Communist Party of North Vietnam, it was agreed that there would be established a front organization directed to destroy the Government of South Vietnam." The grossly misleading character of this "fact," stripped from its context, should be obvious.

promoting discontent with the Government in Saigon and seeking to win supporters for Hanoi." [15] It is documented in the
record of the International Control Commission (see Gettleman, *op. cit.*, pp. 160-190), that from an early date the violations of the Geneva Agreements by the Diem government (in
cooperation with the United States) were both more serious
and numerous than those of North Vietnam.

It is also not generally known in the United States that com-
mando raids *into North Vietnam* were initiated *before 1957*
under the direction of U. S. General Edward Lansdale, Diem's
military adviser in 1954-56; that 3,000 Vietnamese were trained
in Special Forces for raids of this kind; and that recruits under
this program (often Catholic refugees from the North, or former
soldiers in the French army) were sent to Formosa and Guam
for advanced training. [16] The program was small before 1961;
but the Staley-Taylor plan adopted by the Kennedy administration in that year assigned a more important role to com-
mando raids on North Vietnam. After 1961 the number of
commandos captured in North Vietnam increased markedly. [17]
Although the pre-1961 program seems to have been intended
to contribute to the overthrow of the Hanoi regime,[18] the operations both then and later had little success, even as mere harass-
ment raids.

"The waging of guerrilla war by the South Vietnamese in
North Vietnam," Hanson Baldwin has pointed out, "has been

---

[15] *A Threat to the Peace*, p. 3.

[16] Edgar Mowrer, *Réalités*, May 1964; Georges Chaffard, *Le Monde*,
Aug. 7, 1964.

[17] On the post-1961 activities, see Chaffard, *ibid.*; Hanson Baldwin, "U.S. Policy in Vietnam," *New York Times*, Feb. 6, 1964; Peter
Grose ,"Sabotage Flights Hinted in Vietnam," *New York Times*, Dec.
14, 1964; Sergeant Donald Duncan's account of the SOG project, in
Ramparts, Feb. 1966; and General Ky's description of the combat
missions he had flown into North Vietnam before July 1964, and his
statement that the United States was then in the process of training South Vietnamese pilots for "large scale" attacks, in *Ramparts*,
June 1966, p. 14.

completely ineffective. . . . As Mao Tse Tung has written, the guerrilla, to be successful, must swim like a fish in the sea of a friendly populace. The population of North Vietnam, as the few expeditions across the truce line have shown, is unlikely to be friendly." [19]

But if the environment of North Vietnam has not been so conducive to guerrilla warfare as that of the South, the fact remains that efforts were made to stimulate internal disorder in the North by direct military intrusions. What is more, these efforts may be traced to a very early date.

What has been the relative degree of external support for the contending forces in South Vietnam?

The evidence on manpower and material support of the NLF by North Vietnam indicates, first, that prior to the escalation of the war by the United States, the bulk of NLF weapons and supplies were either American or home-made in origin.

In March 1963, General Paul Harkins stated that "the guerrillas are not being reinforced or systematically supplied from North Vietnam, China, or anywhere else. They depend for weapons primarily on what they can capture." [20] A year and a half later, Bernard Fall asserted that "it is estimated that 90 per cent of the weapons being used by the Vietcong are captured American weapons and most of the rest are home-made." [21] The State Department's February 1965 White Paper, when stripped of its rhetoric, shows nothing to conflict with these earlier estimates. Appendix D, which enumerates Communist-bloc manufactured weapons captured from the NLF over an eighteen month period, lists a grand total of 179 weapons. According to Pentagon figures, U. S. and Saigon forces captured an average of 7,500 weapons per 18 month period over the previous three

---

[18] Mowrer and Chaffard, *loc. cit.*   [19] Baldwin, *loc. cit.*

[20] *Washington Post*, March 6, 1963. In fact, not until the middle of 1963, long after the guerrillas had acquired control of most of the countryside, did U.S. Intelligence find any Communist-bloc weapons manufactured after 1954. (Halberstam, "New Red Rifles Used in Vietnam," *New York Times*, July 23, 1963.)

[21] *U.S. News and World Report*, Sept. 28, 1964.

years; thus the 179 Communist-made weapons added up to two per cent of the 18 month average.

The evidence shows, second, that over 90 per cent of the fighters for the NLF have been southerners. In the words of David Halberstam, "The war is largely a conflict of southerners fought on southern land. No capture of North Vietnamese in the south [as of 1964 [22]] has come to light and it is generally believed that most Vietcong weapons have been seized from the South Vietnamese forces." [23] According to Georges Chaffard, in his series on the NLF in *L'Express* in April 1965, "The bulk of the regular units of the NLF today is made up of relatives of the victims of the Diem repression." [24] And Senator Stephen Young stated on January 20, 1966 that both General Westmoreland in South Vietnam and General Stilwell in Thailand had just told him that the war was in essence a civil war, and that over 80 per cent of the NLF were southerners—not infiltrators from the North. Here too the State Department White Paper of February 1965 provides confirmation. Its Appendix C, which examines evidence on the infiltration of North Vietnamese, presents hard proof of exactly *six* individuals who had infiltrated from the North and who had been born there. In fact, the total number of infiltrators claimed for the entire period 1959-1964 was less than the number of U. S. military personnel in South Vietnam at the time of the publication of the White Paper.

Third, it is clear that the provision of military equipment and aid to the Saigon governments by the United States vastly exceeded North Vietnamese aid to the NLF. American aid to Saigon averaged over $500 million per year during the five years preceding the 1965 escalation. In the year that ended on June 30, 1966, U. S. *economic* aid alone totalled approximately

---

[22] It must be pointed out that as early as 1962 direct U.S. participation in the Vietnam fighting was already substantial. "In recent months, one-third to one-half of all air-combat missions, whether in Vietnamese or unmarked planes, have been flown by U.S. pilots." ("The New Metal Birds," *Newsweek*, Oct. 29, 1962.)

[23] *New York Times*, March 23, 1964.

[24] *Viet-Report*, July 1965 (translation).

$675 million—"more than twice as much as was given the previous year, [and] . . . the largest [amount] dispensed to support a single country's economy in any one year since the United States began giving foreign aid in 1948." [25]

These findings suggest two conclusions. First, in terms of weapons, other material aid, and personnel, the Saigon governments were much more dependent on external assistance than the NLF before February 1965. Second, if this is so, it is evidence that the rebels were more closely linked to the native population and were less subject to external control than the U. S.-sustained governments of Saigon.

What is the relative degree of external control over the NLF and the Saigon governments?

There is a tendency on the part of many Americans to neglect the double-edged character of the external control argument. If North Vietnamese control over the NLF can be raised as an issue, why should we disregard the possibility of U. S. control over the Saigon governments? It is well known that Washington hand-picked Diem and played a pivotal role in his overthrow (and in the evolution of the successor cliques). [26] On top of this, the Saigon governments have been more dependent upon American aid—economic and military—than the NLF has been upon its allies. The overpowering physical presence of the United States in South Vietnam gives it a leverage that North Vietnam (or any other Communist power) cannot exercise on the NLF.

The theme of our Appendix 2 would seem to hold good here as well: the Saigon governments show a greater degree of dependence on a foreign power than the NLF or North Vietnam.

Comparatively speaking, what is the degree of popular sup-

---

[25] Eric Pace, *New York Times*, July 2, 1966.

[26] On the rise of Diem, see Robert Scheer, *How the United States Got Involved in Vietnam* (Santa Barbara, Calif., 1965). On the U.S. role in his fall, see Robert Shaplen, *The Lost Revolution* (New York, 1965), ch. vi; Denis Warner, *The Last Confucian* (New York, 1963), ch. 13; Jean Lacouture, *Vietnam Between Two Truces*, pp. 81-87; and David Halberstam, "The Coup in South Vietnam," *New York Times*, Nov. 6, 1963 (reprinted in Gettleman, *Vietnam*).

port in South Vietnam for the NLF *and the U.S.-supported Saigon governments?*

Defenders of American intervention (including Professor Robert Scalapino at the May 1965 Washington Teach-In) tend to avoid this issue by concentrating entirely on the question of the degree of support for the NLF in South Vietnam. They consistently ignore the equally relevant issue of the extent of support for the Saigon governments backed by the United States.

In his remarks before the Senate Foreign Relations Committee on February 17, 1966, General Maxwell Taylor stated that the Ky government "is the first government which is solidly backed *by the armed forces. . . .*" Even this statement (which should be read "higher echelons of officers") has quickly turned out to be an exaggeration, but it is an illuminating reflection of the Johnson administration's dedication to democracy for South Vietnam. Moreover, it probably comes close to exhausting the *domestic* base of the junta. Even in the larger cities of South Vietnam which provide the only support for the Saigon regimes, opposition to the juntas is overwhelming. The bitter hostility to General Ky and his associates manifested by the middle-class students of Saigon; [27] the outbursts of Buddhist and other opposition in the cities, in the face of violent suppression; and the desertion rates and general performance level of the Saigon forces offer grim testimony to that fact. A statement issued by the Roman Catholic Archbishop of Saigon on January 12, 1966 (and completely blacked out by the U.S. press) claimed that the Ky government "is still unable to create a firm legal foundation or obtain the support of the people. This is a most serious obstacle in the path to peace." [28] The extreme minority position of the U.S.-backed military clique also comes through in statements made and positions taken by the junta members. We have already referred to General Ky's frank admission to James Reston "that the Communists are closer to the people's yearnings for social justice and an independent life than his own government." The unyielding opposition of the junta to really

---

[27] Hope Selby, "Vietnamese Students Talk About the War," *New York Times*, Oct. 31, 1965.

[28] London *Observer*, Jan. 23, 1966.

free elections and "their almost desperate desire not to be
pushed into peace negotiations, or even into peace, until they
are more able to compete *politically* with the Vietnamese Communists" tell us much about the relative degree of popular
support for the Saigon government and the NLF.[29]

According to Secretary Rusk, "We have overwhelming evidence from all sections, sectors, areas, groups in South Vietnam
that they do not want what Hanoi is offering to them in South
Vietnam."[30] Once again the Secretary's antennae seem unable
to bring him into touch with reality. If the NLF had no real
support in South Vietnam (and Rusk assumes it is a tool of
Hanoi), it would be incomprehensible why the Saigon regimes,
with heavy U.S. support, lost the *civil* war by the end of 1964.[31]
Further, could the destructive saturation bombing of area after
area make any sense unless it is thought that the ponds volun-
tarily sustaining the NLF must be dried up in order to destroy
the fish? (The alternative explanation is that the United States
is willing to risk alienating the entire rural population in order
to destroy a few floating bands of terrorists.) The truth about
this matter is brought out by an A.P. report on the re-taking
of Binh Ghia village: "The marines, *used to sullen receptions
from villagers in Vietcong controlled areas* [attention Mr. Rusk!],
looked puzzled by the enthusiastic welcome." But this village
was different and unusual; it was settled by Catholic refugees
from the North.[32] Another example of sentiment in the country-

---

[29] Since Ambassador Arthur Goldberg has discovered the NLF to
have the support of only one-half of one per cent of the population
of South Vietnam, and not all of these "voluntary adherents" (*New
York Times*, Feb. 6, 1966), the inability of General Ky to compete
politically with the NLF presents quite a problem.

[30] Transcript of CBS-TV program, Aug. 23, 1965.

[31] Robert Scigliano, a member of the Michigan State University
project group in South Vietnam and supporter of U.S. policy in that
country, states that as early as the end of 1962 U.S. officials in Saigon
estimated that "about one-half of the South Vietnamese support the
National Liberation Front for different reasons, of whom 300,000
are active in their support." (*South Vietnam: Nation Under Stress*,
Boston, 1963, p. 145.)

[32] *Washington Star*, Dec. 30, 1964.

side was furnished by the U.S. "Operation Masher" in January
and February 1966. By U.S. count, 12,000 residents of Binhdinh
province fled their villages during this operation. However,
"when the guns fell silent, 9,000 Vietnamese returned to their
villages—most of which are now again under Vietcong control
—while 3,000 others preferred to stay as refugees under the Government's wing." [33] To reconcile this with the official Washington
theory, it would be necessary to assume that 9,000 of 12,000
Vietnamese passed up their chance to choose "freedom" and
chose instead to return to the rule of "Vietcong terrorism"!

The truth can also be found in many other reports. In May
1966 General Ky made an unscheduled trip to inspect the
scorched earth area in Quang Ngai province "to have a look at
war battered villages wrested recently from Vietcong control.
He made his tour in a U.S. Marine helicopter." His reception
left much to be desired. "He was greeted by silent crowds of
men and women gathered near shell-smashed homes surrounded
by fields sprayed by crop-killing chemicals. In the fortified
village of Duc Phung, Ky distributed American blankets to
silent, expressionless women." [34]

Jack Foisie reported from Saigon that "The area [below
Chu Lai] is now in the hands of Vietnamese pacification teams.
*Unless their efforts to regain the loyalty of the villagers succeed
better than elsewhere*, the Marines will someday have to go back
into the area." [35]

Evidence on NLF support is necessarily imprecise, but the
least that can be said is that "it would be a serious mistake to
consider Communist power in South Vietnam as based predominantly on terrorism or military strength, or even upon the
indifference of an ignorant peasantry. . . . The fact is that
Communism, in the dress of nationalism and its advocacy of
land to the peasants, represents a powerful force in South Vietnam, and one which receives widespread support from the
peasant population." [36]

---

[33] Eric Pace, *New York Times*, July 5, 1966.

[34] *Philadelphia Bulletin*, May 3, 1966.

[35] *Washington Post*, Nov. 7, 1965.

[36] Scigliano, *op. cit.*, p. 158. This "widespread support" was confirmed in the estimate made by the United States Army newspaper

Jean Lacouture has recently described the NLF as "the largest force in South Vietnam." [37] Another French veteran of Vietnam reporting, Max Clos, went a little farther in his statement in the Paris paper, *Le Figaro Littéraire*, March 13, 1965: "All observers [presumably, without an ax to grind] are in agreement on one point: The program and the conduct of the National Liberation Front have won it the adherence, enthusiastic or resigned, of a very large part of the Vietnamese population." A similarly high estimate was given by a North Vietnamese defector, who stated to his captors in early 1965 that the NLF was supported by two-thirds of the population of South Vietnam. [38] On the basis of his Vietnam experiences, Special Forces Master Sergeant Donald Duncan concluded that the growth of the NLF which we have witnessed "is not only impossible without popular support, it actually requires an overwhelming mandate. . . . Little by little, as all these facts made their impact on me, I had to accept the fact that, Communist or not, the vast majority of the people were pro-Viet Cong and anti-Saigon." [39]

The predominant view among informed scholars and journalists is that the NLF has considerable—if not majority—support in South Vietnam. The basis of that support has been the peasantry, who constitute the majority of the population, and to whom the NLF has appealed with three effective arguments.

First, it has fought the political and social dominance of the privileged classes, and it has made land reform a key element

---

in Saigon, *The Observer*, in January 1964, that "some four to five million people support the NLF in varying degrees." Quoted from Bernard Fall, *The Two Vietnams* (New York, 1963), p. 396.

[37] *New York Review of Books*, March 3, 1966.

[38] *New York Times*, May 23, 1965.

[39] *Op cit.* On the explanation of NLF support as a product of terror tactics, Duncan says: "The more often government troops pass through an area, the more surely it would become sympathetic to the Viet Cong. The Viet Cong might sleep in the houses, but the government troops ransacked them. More often than not, the Viet Cong helped plant and harvest the crops; but invariably government troops in the area razed them. Rape is severely punished among the Viet Cong. It is so common among the ARVN that it is seldom reported for fear of even worse atrocities."

of its program. According to Richard Burnham, an American AID official in South Vietnam, "it is still virtually impossible for a child born in a poor rural family to obtain a baccalaureate degree, without which he is permanently relegated to an inferior social position. . . . To these children the Vietcong offers the only real outlet for their energy." [40] (In regard to land reform, the Saigon-based regimes supported by the United States have *never* seriously attempted to win majority favor by radical reform; they have always been linked with the landlord interests. In a recent psychological warfare campaign to "win the people" to the side of the Saigon governments, several hundred million leaflets were dropped over South Vietnam. "Not one of the slips of paper that are being dropped over South Vietnam every day mentions land reform or political or religious liberty or freedom of speech or free enterprise." [41] The peasantry is instead offered anti-Communism, interspersed with napalm.)

Second, popular support for the NLF has been gained by its behavior. Vietcong fighters have deliberately killed thousands of Saigon officials, but the killings have generally been selective. Commonly, those assassinated have been corrupt and brutal Saigon appointees whose death was regarded by the peasantry as desirable.

"Out in the more remote villages of mud and wattle," Denis Warner has pointed out, "the government is identified as the man in uniform who comes on a punitive raid, or with a heavy bodyguard, and who always wants something—money, labor, or even those suspected, sometimes incorrectly, of working for the Vietcong.

"The Viet Cong cadre, on the other hand, is barefooted and dressed in black like every other peasant. He makes tax demands, but they are not excessive. He is meticulous about paying for

---

[40] Charles Mohr, "Saigon Social Ills Worry U.S. Aides," *New York Times*, Feb. 21, 1966. For an account of American aid programs in this Vietnamese setting, see Stanley Andrews, "Red Tape and Broken Promises," *Reporter*, May 5, 1966.

[41] "Saigon Propaganda Enlists Astrology and Song," *New York Times*, Jan. 18, 1966.

food and lodging, and scrupulous also, in his relations with village girls and with the villagers' property."[42]

As so described, NLF behavior is part of the logic of successful guerrilla warfare—and is consistent with the rules of behavior laid down by Mao Tse-Tung and U.S. Special Forces theoreticians.

Third, the NLF has been able to point to the indiscriminate bombings of hundreds of villages and the scorched earth policy carried out by the United States and the Saigon governments. Actions like those have furnished solid proof of the puppet status of Saigon, and of the fact that the NLF is a nationalist group fighting for independence against a powerful foreign aggressor.

Conclusion. From the standpoint of six critical issues bearing on the charge of aggression—the failure to hold unifying elections in 1956, other major violations of the Geneva Accords, the indigenous origins of the conflict in South Vietnam, the chief sources of expansion of the conflict, the relative amounts of external support for the contending parties in South Vietnam, and the degree of native support for the NLF and the Saigon governments—the verdict would appear to be this: the conflict in South Vietnam is civil in nature, with the United States as the only major outside participant. The escalation of the war by the Johnson administration has transformed the United States from an interventionist in a civil war into an open aggressor nation.

---

[42] *The Last Confucian,* p. 32. On assassinations by the Vietcong, see also Senator Robert Kennedy's International Police Academy speech of July 9, 1965 (reprinted in *Congressional Record,* July 22, 1965).

APPENDIX 4

GENOCIDE IN VIETNAM?

On December 9, 1948, the Genocide Convention of the United Nations General Assembly defined genocide as

"Any of the following acts committed with intent to destroy, in whole or in part, a national, ethnical, racial, or religious group, as such:

"(a) Killing members of the group;

"(b) Causing serious bodily or mental harm to members of the group;

"(c) Deliberately inflicting on the group conditions of life calculated to bring about its physical destruction in whole or in part . . ."

A common reaction among Americans to the news that our armed forces are killing innocent civilians in Vietnam is: "Well, of course that's deplorable, but innocent people die in every war and this one is no different." Unfortunately, this war *is* different —so much so that the ultimate logic of American military policy in Vietnam appears to be genocide, in terms of the above definition.[1]

The Logic of a War of Extermination

First of all, in South Vietnam American military methods are not being employed to liberate people from foreign forces which can be relatively isolated from the native population, as were the German armies in France and Belgium during the Liberation of 1944. On the contrary, these methods are being used to combat guerillas who cannot be separated from the underlying Vietnamese peasantry. U.S. forces have consequently been placed in the position of trying to find and kill soldiers and irregulars who are part of the native population itself. Furthermore, only

---

[1] See also Gordon Zahn, "The Crime of Silence. Are We Accomplices in Mass-Murder in Vietnam?" *Commonweal,* June 17, 1966.

with the support of the population can the guerillas continue to exist and fight. This situation is generally recognized; in fact, several advocates of American policy in Vietnam have acknowledged, reluctantly, that the Vietnamese peasantry forms the base of the guerilla movement and provides widespread support for it.

Second, since the native peasantry is the backbone of the NLF and furnishes most of its manpower, food, and information, that *entire group* gradually becomes the target of American military actions—which have thus evolved into virtually unrestrained warfare *against the entire Vietnamese peasantry*. That much is made unmistakably clear by the systematic, massive use of the most modern firepower against innumerable peasant villages, the deliberate burning to the ground of peasant homes in village after village, and the spray killing of food crops by chemical means in strongly NLF areas.[2] In the eyes of U.S. commanders, destroying the peasant base of the guerilla movement is not brutality for its own sake; it is simply the most efficient means of achieving the desired military victory. This view is reflected in a statement by a high U.S. field commander, reported from Saigon as saying that "If the people are to the guerillas as the oceans are to the fish, then . . . we are going to dry up that ocean."[3]

---

[2] This program of chemical warfare violates international law in its own right, but it is now openly acknowledged and under expansion in 1966. (*New York Times*, Dec. 21, 1965; March 10 and July 26, 1966.) Dr. Jean Mayer of the Harvard School of Public Health has pointed out that chemical destruction of rice crops and grain stores *always* affects small children, the elderly, and other "innocent bystanders" much more than enemy troops; see *Science*, April 15, 1966, p. 291.

[3] U.P.I. dispatch, quoted in *New Statesman*, March 11, 1966.
This purely military view is also illustrated by comments of a U.S. helicopter officer to the *New York Times'* Jack Langguth (Sept. 19, 1965). According to the officer, the only way to defeat the Vietcong is "terror." "We must terrorize the villagers even more [than the Vietcong], so they see that their real self-interest lies with us . . . Terror is what it takes."
See also the equally candid statement by an American official in Saigon, in an interview with Robert Guillain (*Le Monde*, May 26–June 1, 1966): "[There are] three choices for the peasants: stay where they are; come into the areas controlled by us; flee into the

Third, what makes such warfare feasible—and even attractive —is that the United States has the military power and technique to pursue it, while the other side does not. It is questionable whether any other war in history has seen such an incredible imbalance of firepower. In a real sense, the Johnson administration's escalation of the war in 1965 was directly related to this imbalance. Escalation represented Washington's decision to nullify the loss of the civil war in South Vietnam by changing the rules of the game: by imposing on Vietnam a new brand of war in which the United States has an overwhelming advantage. The new, expanding war revolves about the methodical deployment of firepower, dispensed by equipment and in amounts which no other power in the world can hope to match.

In sum, the logic of American military escalation leads to nothing less than a war of extermination against the native Vietnamese peasantry: because the guerillas cannot be segregated from the peasantry; because the peasantry provides the necessary broad base for the guerillas; and because the United States has the military means to eradicate this base completely, if need be, to create an "independent" South Vietnam.

Drying up the ocean, as suggested by the U.S. commander quoted above, is "deliberately inflicting on the group [the peasant majority of South Vietnam] conditions of life calculated to bring about its physical destruction in whole or in part." The results are genocidal, and they fall into the same category whether the goal is the planned killing of entire groups on principle (as in the Nazi extermination of the Jews) or whether the killing is done instead for political reasons because a group stands in the way of some chosen objective (as in the U.S. drive to achieve an "independent" South Vietnam, whatever the cost).

Basically, such a campaign of extermination is a logical product of Western-type war-making applied to guerilla movements broadly supported by the native population. An added, fateful

---

interior, into Vietcong zones. The application of our air power . . . aims at rendering the first choice impossible, the second attractive, and the third reduced to zero." Thus, application of this theory is chiefly through American airstrikes, "the largest single cause of that insecurity" in the Vietnamese countryside. (Charles Mohr, *New York Times*, Sept. 5, 1965 and Aug. 16, 1966.)

result of its methods is that their indiscriminate character often drives the population into the arms of the insurgents faster. For years observers in Vietnam have pointed out this counter-productive "feedback" effect.[4] The Pentagon itself estimates that the NLF has grown more since the escalation of the war than in any earlier period.

"But—here is the catch—this [feedback effect] seems to be exactly what the Army and the Air Force want. Why? Because once every peasant in a given area is considered a Vietcong, then the planes and helicopters can at last be used to their full extent in that area. Since everybody is an enemy, everyone and everything becomes a target. This is not intentional brutality; rather it is the reflex of the military mind . . . [which] immediately sets about converting the situation into one it can understand. From the military standpoint it makes more sense to turn the entire population into an enemy and wipe them all out, than to undertake the delicate task of responding to the legitimate complaints and legitimate aspirations of the Vietnamese population."[5]

This interaction between (1) the systematic destruction and killing carried on by U.S. forces, and (2) the feedback of additional recruits to the NLF, reinforces the conclusion that genocide is the limit to the escalation process at work in Vietnam.

---

[4] "When you bomb a village of 3,000 people which perhaps five Vietcong have infiltrated, you are going to create a lot more than five Vietcong by the time you have finished."—Roger Hilsman, former Assistant Secretary of State for Far Eastern Affairs.

More graphic is the testimony of former Master Sergeant Donald Duncan: "One day I asked one of our Vietnamese helicopter pilots what he thought of the last bomb raid. 'I think maybe today we make many Vietcong.'" (*Ramparts*, Feb. 1966.) Earlier remarks to the same effect were those of Nguyen Lac Hoa, the priest who organized the force called the "sea swallows" to fight the NLF. "When it [the war] is fought as an international war, we have no chance to win. How can we explain to a mother when her son is burned by napalm? And how can we expect a young man to fight for us when his aged father was killed by artillery fire? Indeed, how can we claim to be with the people when we burn their homes simply because those houses happen to be in the Vietcong-controlled territory?" (*New York Times*, Sept. 1, 1964.)

[5] Martin Nicolaus, in *Viet-Report*, Aug.-Sept. 1965.

The Record: Testimony and Statistics

There is by now a voluminous record of incidents inevitable in a war waged against a native population: U.S. troops unleashing large quantities of expendable ordnance against "snipers" and "Vietcong villages" and finding later—often to their own dismay—that they have killed more women and children than "Vietcong." [6] Applications of open-ended quantities of bullets, shells, bombs, rockets, napalm, phosphorous, and gasses against "Vietcong areas" and "suspected Vietcong strongholds" must necessarily take a staggering toll of civilian life and property. George Kennan surely had that in mind when he stated before the Senate Foreign Relations Committee (February 10, 1966):

"Any total rooting out of the Vietcong from the territory of South Vietnam could be achieved, if it could be achieved at all, only at the cost of a degree of damage to civilian life and of civilian suffering generally, for which I would not like to see this country responsible."

Any measurement of the civilian toll would of course be imprecise, but the problem is aggravated by the understandable reluctance of U.S. authorities to estimate or report civilian casualties. However, other sources of information do exist, and they sketch a picture of human agony unsurpassed since World War II.

For statistics of wounded, one estimate may be made from what a U.S. Medical Corps colonel told British reporter Nicholas Tomalin: that the civilian to Vietcong wounded ratio has been four to one. [7] The great majority of those wounded civilians are victims of American firepower. Bernard Fall has indicated that the admission statistics of American and South Vietnamese hospitals show between 30 and 40 Vietnamese civilians treated for wounds inflicted by our weapons for each civilian wounded by Vietcong fire. [8] But in addition, it must be kept in mind that these hospital statistics exclude thousands of wounded. Accord-

---

[6] See, for example, Eric Norden, "American Atrocities in Vietnam," *Liberation*, Feb. 1966, pp. 6-9.

[7] London *Sunday Times*, June 5, 1966.

[8] *New York Review of Books*, March 17, 1966.

ing to Neil Sheehan of the *New York Times* (November 30, 1965):

"Each month 600 to 1,000 civilians wounded by bombs, shells, bullets and napalm are brought to the provincial hospital in Quangngai town . . . A recent visitor to the hospital found several children lying on cots, their bodies horribly burned by napalm.

"Officials believe that a majority of the civilian war wounded never get to the hospital because of a lack of transportation or because they live in areas still controlled by the Vietcong."

Sheehan's information was later confirmed by French reporter Robert Guillain, who was told by a Vietnamese doctor at another hospital: "Those you see here are those who were able to come. For every one who can reach a town, there are 10 who die in the village or the fields or wherever they are struck. This is true above all of the badly burned." [9]

For statistics of civilians killed, *New York Times* reporter Charles Mohr wrote (September 5, 1965) that "This is strategic bombing in a friendly, allied country . . . no one here seriously doubts that significant numbers of innocent civilians are dying every day in South Vietnam." Representative Clement Zablocki stated, after a visit to Vietnam in February 1966, that the average ratio of civilian to Vietcong killed was two to one, and that in some "search and destroy" operations, the ratio has reached six to one. [10] Such testimony would indicate that civilian deaths from American firepower must number in the hundreds of thousands. And such indications are borne out by observers familiar with the war. Hugh Campbell, former Canadian member of the International Control Commission, estimated the total number of civilians killed in Vietnam between 1961 and 1964 at 160,000. [11] For 1965 alone, Robert Guillain estimated that 100,000 civilians were killed. [12]

For overall casualties (killed and wounded) there are fewer estimates. One—consistent with both the wounded and killed ratios cited above—was offered by Dr. Wyan Washburn, who

---

[9] *Le Monde*, March 12, 1966.

[10] *New York Times*, March 17, 1966.

[11] *Buffalo Evening News*, Jan. 30, 1965.

[12] Reported by Alexander Werth, in *The Nation*, June 13, 1966.

has served on an American rural health council project in Vietnam: "People who know estimate that the civilian-versus-soldier casualties in the war are running about ten-to-one." [13] If we multiply by ten official U.S. figures for Vietcong casualties since 1961 (260,000), we arrive at 2.6 million civilian casualties—one-sixth of the population of South Vietnam. If the Vietcong casualty figure is reduced by as much as 30 per cent to account for probable exaggeration, the smaller figure multiplied by ten gives 1.8 million casualties—one-eighth of the population. Inexact as it must be, this arithmetic still is bound to give some idea of the magnitude of the destruction of the Vietnamese peasantry.

In all likelihood, the situation will worsen. Even greater firepower is to be brought to bear on NLF forces, and thus on the civilian population of which they are an integral part. Secretary of Defense MacNamara has promised "massive new increases" in firepower and preparations to "support a much higher rate" of ordnance consumption. [14] This statement portends a level of escalation of almost indescribable violence and destruction, particularly since *present* rates of ordnance consumption already border on the unimaginable. American forces are now using at least 83 million rounds of small arms ammunition per month, and, per year, 10 million mortar and artillery rounds, 2 million bombs, [15] 4.8 million rockets, 6.8 million grenades. [16] It must be repeated that these figures are only annual rates as of early 1966; they are certain to increase.

A quantitative, mechanistic approach to problem-solving is the famous trade-mark of Secretary MacNamara. Applied to the use of firepower to destroy the NLF, it leads to genocidal

---

[13] *American Medical Association News*, May 2, 1966.

[14] *New York Times*, Jan. 21, 1966.

[15] In its bombings, the U.S. Air Force was using 50,000 tons of bombs per month as of March 1966. Compare that with an average of 17,000 tons of bombs per month for the 37 months of the Korean War and an average of 48,000 tons per month used during World War II in the African and European theaters *combined*. Yet this rate will also increase. (*New York Times*, April 21, 1966, report of MacNamara's testimony.)

[16] John Maffre, *Washington Post*, Feb. 11, 1966; *Business Week*, March 5, 1966.

warfare—a concept which MacNamara may well be incapable of understanding. The Secretary told Professor Henry Graff that General Westmoreland would not need to use all this power: "I can't imagine he's going to find targets to fire all this stuff at." [17] One can only wonder whether MacNamara fails to understand, among other things, the effects of the "open target area" policy followed by his forces, where "an aircraft unable to dispose of its explosives on the planned target may drop them at will on a village, rice paddy, man or beast, wherever it suits the pilot's fancy." [18] One might also ask whether the Secretary knows of or understands the implications of the most recent case of traditional U.S. inter-service rivalry—in this case, a contest between the U.S. Air Force and Navy to fly the most bombing missions in South Vietnam, a contest that has resulted in "many relatively unimportant targets bombed." [19]

American military authorities are not ignorant of the dilemma created by escalation and the wholesale killing it engenders. In October 1965, General Westmoreland received the report of a "special board on air firepower" which recommended that "in most cases South Vietnamese villages should not be bombed from the air before the villagers have been warned to leave the area . . . The restraint would apply even in cases where 'light' ground fire was received from the village." General Westmoreland was expected to accept the board's recommendation, "but the report of the committee is still being studied and refined." [20]

However, it is scarcely even pretended that any efforts are made to protect or warn the civilian populations. In fact, that would be contrary to the very logic of "search and kill," since such warnings would be incompatible with effective hot pursuit; they would require an ability to weigh short-term military suc-

---

[17] *New York Times,* March 20, 1966.

[18] Stephen Cary, in *Progressive,* Oct. 1965. Bernard Fall corroborated Cary's account of this policy, in his description of the "free bomb zone" of some 300 square miles around Zone D north of Saigon; *Ramparts,* Dec. 1965.

[19] C.B.S., *World News Report,* April 20, 1966.

[20] "Warning of Air Raids Urged in Vietnam," Charles Mohr, *New York Times,* Oct. 14, 1965.

cess against longer term political consequences of actions—a
skill which has normally eluded the American decision makers
in Vietnam. The fate of General Westmoreland's "special board
on firepower" and its recommendations may be judged by the
answer given to Robert Guillain in February 1966 when he asked
U.S. military officials what proportion of the reported 700 Vietcong killed in "Operation Masher" were civilians: "In a Vietcong
area like that one, civilians and military are all the same." [21]

---

[21] *Le Monde*, Feb. 24-March 2, 1966. This is by no means a new
attitude. In November 1964 a U.S. helicopter crew told Jean Lacouture that in the countryside "all that moves must be considered
as Vietcong"; *Vietnam between Two Truces*, p. 163. Earlier, an
American helicopter pilot spoke similarly to author Richard Tre-
gaskis (*Vietnam Diary*, New York, 1963, p. 108): "Down there
you have pretty solid VC [Vietcong] areas, where you can assume
everybody is an enemy. You know, the 362 [the 362d Squadron,
which preceded the pilot's unit in Vietnam] were wild men. One
*chopper would go first, and when the people would go running,
the second plane would spray 'em.*"
  Charles Mohr described a U.S. Navy airstrike against the Delta
hamlet of Phuong Hiep: "Rockets flashed as they struck . . . and
the deadly surf of napalm splashed through the village. There
were also big general purpose bombs. 'I wonder if any civilians
were killed?' a pilot was asked. 'Who the hell knows?' was the
answer." (*New York Times*, Sept. 5, 1965.)
  For further information about the problem of genocide see:
  Bernard Fall, "Blitz in Vietnam," *New Republic*, Oct. 9, 1965,
and "Vietnam Album," *Ramparts*, Dec. 1965; "Bombing South Vietnam," *New York Times* editorial, Nov. 21, 1965; "Bombes sur les
villages," by Robert Guillain, *Le Monde*, May 26-June 1, 1966; "The
'Weed Killers.' Chemical and Biological Warfare in Vietnam," by
Carol Brightman, *Viet-Report*, June-July 1966; Neil Sheehan,
"Unnoted Victims: Vietnam Peasants," *New York Times*, Feb. 15,
1966; the description of the American naval and air destruction of
five fishing hamlets at Duchai, "Rubble Depicts the Agony of a
Town in Vietnam," by Sheehan, *New York Times*, Nov. 30, 1965;
the report of the drowning of up to 200 civilians from a passenger
boat sunk in the Saigon River by U.S. aircraft "in error," because
the pilots said there was "no basis" for believing the boat was not
a Vietcong boat ("Saigon Says U.S. Helicopters Sank Vessel Carry-
ing Civilians," *New York Times*, Jan. 13, 1966); Charles Mohr's
New York Times report (Jan. 28, 1966) of one day's work by
American aircraft in South Vietnam—the destruction of "3530 Vietcong structures"; the bombardment by U.S. planes, using phosphor-

ous and fragmentation bombs, of the friendly village of De Duc in late October 1965: 103 villagers were killed and wounded in this attack, which presumably would not have been reported had the village simply been classified as a "Vietcong village" (*Manchester Guardian Weekly*, Nov. 4, 1965, and *New York Times*, Nov 1, 1965); the accounts of the three U.S. bombings and strafings in eight weeks of the demilitarized zone between North and South Vietnam —also "in error" (and with heavy civilian casualties), *Philadelphia Inquirer*, Sept. 18, 1965, and *New York Times*, Nov. 14, 1965; and the acknowledgment by the U.S. military command in Saigon that incidents involving civilian casualties from American firepower had reached *"epic proportions"* ("Westmoreland Calls Civilian Toll Great Problem," *New York Times*, Aug. 25, 1966).

See lastly "U.S. Troops in Delta Begin Scorched Earth Policy," A.P. dispatch from Saigon, Jan. 6, 1966:

"For years Americans refused to participate in 'scorched earth' efforts, leaving them to the Vietnamese. Now Americans are directly involved.

"The intensely cultivated flat lands south of the Vaico Oriental River about 20 miles from Saigon are prime 'scorched earth' targets. U.S. paratroopers from the 173rd Airborne Brigade began operating there last weekend.

"They burned to the ground every hut they saw. Sampans were sunk and bullock carts were smashed. The 173rd laid their base camp among the blackened frames of burned houses. Within two miles of the camp not a house was left standing . . .

"Every house found by the 173rd was burned to the ground. Every cooking utensil was smashed, every banana tree severed, every mattress slashed . . . Thousands of ducks and chickens were slaughtered . . . Dozens of pigs, water buffalo and cows were destroyed. A twenty mile stretch along the Vaico Oriental was left scorched and barren . . . The province chief [a Saigon official] had told the Americans that *every man south of the river was a Vietcong*."

"The credibility of the United States government has been one of the numerous casualties of the war in Vietnam . . . Mistaken judgments are understandable—though if too frequent, indefensible; but deliberate distortion or obfuscation, or the selection or repression of facts for propaganda purposes, is inexcusable. Americans are dying in Vietnam and more will die; there should be no misunderstanding whatsoever about what they are dying for or why."—New York Times, April 23, 1965.

* * * *

"There is a big 'confidence gap' today between Mr. Mc-Namara and key Senate and House leaders in the fields of military and foreign policy who do not share President Johnson's faith in his Defense Secretary. . . . [It is] largely the result of heavy-handed Pentagon censorship of questions raised by Congress about the nation's military preparedness and Mr. McNamara's emotional outburst last week in answering charges that the Vietnam war has stretched thin the nation's military manpower and equipment."—Jack Steele, Scripps-Howard writer, Washington Daily News, March 7, 1966.

* * * *

"The President's latest problem is one of fading public confidence in official government pronouncements on the conduct of U.S. diplomacy in Vietnam. Indeed, Washington is having trouble maintaining both at home and abroad the kind of credibility needed to support its political position. It is this loss of confidence that now gives rise to doubts and even suspicions about whether the Administration really means what is being said . . ."—Richard Reston, Washington correspondent, Los Angeles Times, Dec. 29, 1965.

* * * *

"The essential veracity of an American government has seldom been a prolonged case of doubt. This is why persistent charges of a 'credibility gap' in the Johnson Administration merit examination."—James Deakin, White House correspondent of the St. Louis Post-Dispatch, in the New Republic, Jan. 29, 1966.

* * * *

"There are times when lying is justified."—Malcolm Kildnuff, Assistant Press Secretary for Presidents Kennedy and Johnson, in an address before the Texas Public Relations Association, Sept. 9, 1966.

"A government, like a man, can be caught in only a few misrepresentations before people refuse to believe anything it says. Much of the current clamor against the U.S. Vietnamese policy is probably based in just such a feeling. A democratic government has a moral obligation to be candid with its citizens; and lack of candor poisons the open discussion often necessary to sound policy and public support. But even from the narrow viewpoint of its own self-interest, the Administration should recognize that its credibility is a precious but easily expendable asset."—Wall Street Journal, Dec. 1, 1965.

* * * *

"News management in the nation's capital is currently more deliberate and sweeping than it ever was during World War II or the Korean period . . . Before the wellsprings of public discussion are further damaged or dried up, the Johnson Administration urgently needs to recognize that there is no point trying to win the world while doing irreparable injury here at home."—Doris Fleeson, Washington Evening Star, May 4, 1965.

* * * *

"I believe that frankness and candor on the part of the administration is absolutely essential."—Vice President Hubert Humphrey, CBS, May 20, 1966.

* * * *

"An official is a man by definition doing the public business. The public has a right, and the public has a need, to know about its business . . . The truth is that practices have grown up in the American government in the last years—and particularly quite recently—of a kind that amount to an unseen and . . . extremely unhealthy change in the basic American system.

"Our government . . . lives and moves and acts by public information. It does not matter what an inner group of policymakers may decide. If the public is not adequately informed, if they do not understand the problem, the decisions that the policymakers make will not be publicly supported, and so the job will not be done."—Joseph Alsop, in speech before the American Foreign Service Association, March 25, 1965.

* * * *

"President Johnson grandly mixes truth, half-truth and non-truth, and dares you to attempt to isolate them."—Douglas Kiker, White House correspondent of the New York Herald-Tribune, quoted in The Diplomat, April 1966.

"I am sure that the great American people, if only they knew the true facts and background to the developments in South Vietnam, will agree with me that further bloodshed is unnecessary . . . As you know, in times of war and hostilities, the first casualty is truth."—U Thant, Secretary-General of the United Nations, Feb. 1965.

* * * *

"A steady stream of misinformation about the war in Vietnam is reaching the American people."—Charles Mohr in dispatch from Saigon, New York Times, Nov. 26, 1965.

* * * *

"If a government repeatedly resorts to lies in crises where lies seem to serve its interests best, it will one day be unable to employ the truth effectively when truth would serve its interests best. A government that too readily rationalizes its right to lie in a crisis will never lack for either lies or crises." J. Russell Wiggins, editor of the Washington Post, in his book Freedom or Secrecy (1966).

* * * *

"No single factor is more important to the strength of our democracy than the free flow of accurate information about the government's operation. The citizen in a democracy must know what his government is doing, or he will lack the soundest basis for judging the candidates and the platforms of our political parties."—Clark Mollenhoff, Washington correspondent of the Cowles Publications, in his book Washington Cover-up (1962).

* * * *

"You don't have to indulge in prevarication and falsehoods to create a credibility gap."—Senator Everett M. Dirksen, Senate Republican leader, quoted in the Washington Post, June 28, 1966.

* * * *

"President [Johnson] has exhibited something approaching genius in creating contrived, if not spurious, public impressions about himself and his actions."—Tom Wicker, Washington Bureau Chief, New York Times, quoted in Harpers, June 1965.

* * * *

"All government handouts lie; some lie more than others."—Joseph Alsop, quoted in The Opinionmakers (1966) by William Rivers.

"... it's inherent in government's right to lie to save itself when it's going up into nuclear disaster. This seems to me basic—basic ... I do not expect virtue to come out of men—complete virtue—or even 75 percent virtue. If any of us are virtuous 51 percent of the time in life, it's a good record and in politics an amazing record."—Arthur Sylvester, Assistant Secretary of Defense for Public Affairs, Dec. 6, 1962.

* * * *

"But there is growing doubt concerning the President's [Johnson's] candor ... Not only are many Americans not comforted by what they are being told—in many instances they do not believe it. This so-called 'credibility gap' has become an issue in itself, possibly the biggest one confronting Lyndon Johnson.—Life, Aug. 12, 1966.

* * * *

"High Johnson administration officials no longer hide their fears about a possible 'crisis of confidence' in the U.S. government at home and abroad ... To put it bluntly, the administration has been caught on several occasions denying things that were true or explaining them with partial truths, the corollary of which is partial lies."—R. H. Shackford, Scripps-Howard writer, Dec. 21, 1965.

* * * *

"The 'credibility gap' which has affected the Johnson Administration's pronouncements on Vietnam appears to have spread to this part of the world. A few West German officials still profess to know what U.S. policy here is going to be over the next year, but even these officials show no great confidence in their beliefs. ... The trouble is that ... the Administration has been saying one thing one day, doing something else on the next ... Wild rumors proliferate in all directions, and most of them seem to have some official source. The impression is strong that either the United States is playing it by ear from day to day, without making up its mind on any of these issues, or else that so many different minds in the Administration have been made up that nobody really knows which one counts."—Anatole Shub, Washington Post, dispatch from Bonn, May 7, 1966.

* * * *

"We have had a great problem here maintaining our credibility with our own people."—Arthur J. Goldberg, U.S. Ambassador to the United Nations, Dec. 19, 1965.